How to grow
NATIVE
ORCHIDS
IN GARDENS LARGE
AND SMALL

How to grow
NATIVE
ORCHIDS
IN GARDENS LARGE
AND SMALL

The comprehensive
guide to cultivating
local species

Wilson Wall
Dave Morgan

Published by
Green Books
An imprint of UIT Cambridge Ltd
www.greenbooks.co.uk

PO Box 145, Cambridge CB4 1GQ, England
+44 (0)1223 302 041

First published in 2019, in England.

Wilson Wall and Dave Morgan have asserted their moral rights under the
Copyright, Designs and Patents Act 1988.

The illustrations on the front cover and in the interior are by Dave Morgan.

All interior photographs are by the authors, with the exception of Figures 0.1, 0.2
and 0.4 on pages 17-18, and the following: Pages 12-13, 28, 84, 150: Stuart Smith.
Page 19: Usunderberg. Endpapers and Pages 72-73, 100, 123, 152 (Fig 9.5): Yvette
Verner. Page 77: Simon Rose. Pages 86 (Fig 4.10 and Fig. 4.12) and 151 (Fig 9.3):
Ashwood Nurseries. Page 70: Shutterstock. Page 131: Lawnfl ite.
Page 151 (Fig 9.2): Adrian and Rhianon Wheeler.

The publisher has endeavoured to identify all copyright
holders, but will be glad to correct in future editions
any omissions brought to its notice.

Design by Jayne Jones.

ISBN: 978 0 85784 460 6 (hardback)
ISBN: 978 0 85784 461 3 (epub)
ISBN: 978 0 85784 462 0 (PDF)
ISBN: 978 0 85784 464 4 (Kindle)

Disclaimer: the advice herein is believed to be correct at the
time of printing, but the author and publisher accept no
liability for actions inspired by this book.

10 9 8 7 6 5 4 3 2 1

FSC
www.fsc.org
MIX
Paper from
responsible sources
FSC® C016779

Contents

Acknowledgements

Wilson sends thanks to the ever supportive and enthusiastic Alison, also to Simon Rose and Adrian and Rhiannon Wheeler for the photographs of their gardens. Dave would like to thank his wife, Val, for her forbearance during the hours he spent hidden away painting and looking for orchids to photograph.

We would both like to thank everyone at Green Books and especially our editor, Alethea Doran, who diligently tracked down inconsistencies and errors and was so tenacious in making us put them right.

Opposite: Common Spotted Orchid (*Dactylorhiza fuchsii*).

Introduction

Having native orchids growing in the garden must be the dream of every gardener who has ever come across a wild-flower meadow rich with orchids and butterflies on a beautiful summer's day. As this book will help you discover, native orchids are neither difficult to cultivate nor require special conditions to thrive, and while a large meadow may be beyond the reach of most, the corner of a garden lawn can provide the perfect setting for naturalized orchids.

Even without a garden you can grow orchids. A small but spectacular show can be created in pots on a patio, in a courtyard or even on a balcony. If you have access to any outdoor space at all, whether in shade or sun, there will be a species of native orchid that can grow and thrive there.

There are good reasons for growing native orchids, beyond the simple aesthetic one of how lovely they look. Many wild orchid species are now rare. Even species such as the Common Twayblade or Common Spotted Orchid, while locally abundant in a small area, cannot really be called common any more. This stems from the extraordinary life cycle of an orchid, whose complex development from seed requires the presence of a fungus in the soil. The orchid and the fungus have such a close, symbiotic relationship that without the fungus, the orchid seeds cannot germinate in the wild.

With some orchid species, this dependency is very specific - for example, the Greater Butterfly Orchid is associated only with the fungus *Tulasnella calospora* - while others are less fussy. Given this precarious association, it is perhaps not surprising that orchids have a long, slow journey from seed to flowering plant.

The time it takes for orchids to flower in the wild is their downfall, as any disturbance during their development can cause the untimely collapse of a wild population. Changes in land use, such as ploughing and the application of herbicides, are the main threats. In sites of particular interest, pressure from visitors inadvertently treading on plants can also cause damage.

When you grow orchids in your garden, you are providing them with a protected environment in which they can flourish undisturbed. Once established, your orchids will become a self-perpetuating colony and in a small but significant way you will be helping to boost the population of the species. If you live in the suburbs, where wind can distribute the seeds

Opposite: Early Marsh Orchid (*Dactylorhiza incarnata*).
Right: Northern Marsh Orchid (*Dactylorhiza purpurella*).

across several gardens, the orchids may spread further, enhancing your whole area. No doubt there will be surprise and pride when the neighbours discover that an exquisite wild orchid has appeared in their garden.

Decline in our native orchids has been going on for a long time, but even in the mid-twentieth century some species were so common they were considered nothing special. The Green-winged Orchid, for example, was described as one of the most common orchids of England and Wales. Today, many people have never seen a Green-winged Orchid, and the remaining populations are scattered; geographically isolated in old pastures and genetically separated from each other. This decline continues as an inevitable result of changes in agriculture, with our traditional meadows largely replaced by barren pasture required for high milk production.

The sad depletion of orchid populations is evocatively illustrated in this passage from *Through the Woods* by HE Bates (1936). Here he describes the Greater Butterfly Orchid, which he remembers from his childhood during the 1920s:

For me they are reminders of great occasions, of drowsy midsummer afternoons when we walked, in order to visit my aunt at her pub in Bedfordshire, through the woods where they grew and where, I hope, they still grow. That wood, a small square wood remarkable for only one other thing, was drenched with the exotic, almost tropical scent of hundreds of those ghostly orchis [sic].

He never tells us exactly where the wood is, but we would be amazed if summer evenings were still drenched with the scent of Butterfly Orchids. However, we can recreate this scene in our own gardens, in a shady little area of magic. Growing your own native orchids may seem a small step in halting their decline, but it will be a powerful statement that you care about what happens in the natural world and have done something positive about it.

Orchids are one of the most exciting things you can have growing in the garden. As well as adding a brightness and dignity, they attract many different insects, such as long-tongued moths, which are especially keen to visit Butterfly Orchids in the early evening, to sip nectar and pollinate the flowers. Growing native orchids outdoors is all about diversity; it isn't just about these species in isolation but about the associated plants that are part of a natural ecosystem.

The very special relationship between orchids and their habitat, their ecological position in the world, is what makes them so valuable as a marker of the health of an environment - and why it is so important that we help to nurture them.

Southern Marsh Orchid (*Dactylorhiza praetermissa*).

HOW TO USE THIS BOOK

The book starts with the history and botany of orchids and builds up to the practical how-to and the inspirational can-do. If, like us, you get bitten by the orchid bug, you may wish to read it from start to finish. But it is also designed to be dipped in and out of at any point; to be used as a guide as you develop your own garden orchid display. Depending on your level of ambition, some sections may appeal more than others: for example, Chapter 4 explains the basics of growing orchids, while Chapter 5 covers growing orchids from seed in culture, which is a technical process and takes some practice.

In Part 1, the first two chapters provide a bit of background to understanding orchids and how they came to be regarded so highly. There are many orchids native to Britain and Ireland, and several are easy to grow. Chapter 3 includes a full list of our native species and explains which we recommend for cultivation and which may be worth trying. Full descriptions are given, including accounts of their natural habitats.

Part 2 covers cultivation and care, including a section in Chapter 4 on container gardening with orchids. Part 3 looks at the different types of setting in which you might naturalize orchids in your garden - whether a garden meadow, a patch of trees or a boggy area, or a rockery as an option for chalk-hill species. In each case we give suggestions for native companion plants to complement your orchids and help create a beautiful and thriving habitat. The last chapter brings all of this together, inspiring you to breathe new life into a wild area by reintroducing native orchids.

A NOTE ON NAMES

Throughout this book we have mostly referred to orchids and other plants by their common name. Please see the Plant Lists (pages 166-9) for a list of common and Latin names. For clarity, orchid common names have capital initials.

Whatever your level of interest, we hope this book will encourage you to cherish these remarkable flowers and help them flourish.

Heath Spotted Orchid (*Dactylorhiza maculata*).

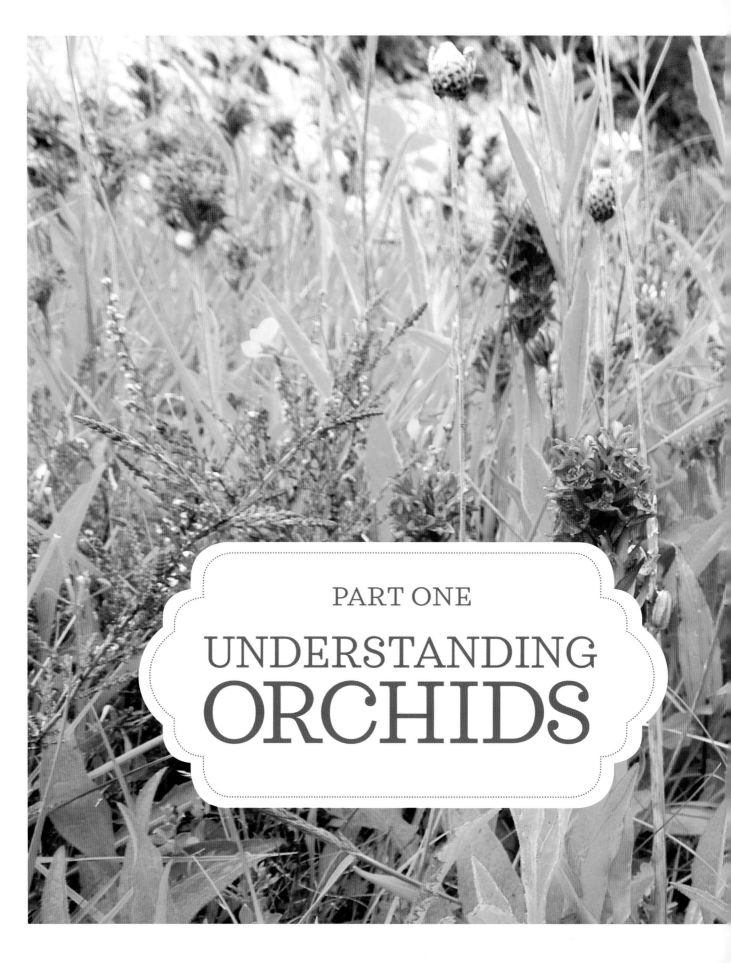

PART ONE

UNDERSTANDING ORCHIDS

A love affair with ORCHIDS

Whether it is the shape of the flower, the colours or the rarity, orchids hold a fascination for us all. In Northern Europe these special plants are indicators of a healthy meadow, the flower standing proud in a splash of colour shouting "Look at me - I am an orchid!" We became enchanted by orchids, first by impressive tropical blooms and then by more subtle native flowers, once growers realised they were the same plant and that these apparently different flowers have a common shape, consistent across all orchid species, regardless of size or where they come from.

Opposite: Early Purple Orchid (*Orchis mascula*) with bluebell (*Hyacinthoides non-scripta*) and male-fern (*Dryopteris filix-mas*). Woodland in mid-May.

A BRIEF HISTORY OF ORCHID DISCOVERY

Although this book is about cultivation of native orchids in the garden, the broader history of these plants is fascinating and worth a short digression. It has involved explorers, fortunes, skullduggery, maps written in code and amazing stories of chance.

Orchid-growing in Britain started with the collection of the large and blowsy tropical types, which were brought back as botanical samples. Native orchids were regarded as common wild flowers and few people realized that they were botanically identical to the exotic orchids, only smaller.

Trade in tropical orchids started in the seventeenth century, when these beautiful flowers captured the imagination of the public. Great efforts were made to transport live plants, with limited success, and it was a long time before any serious attempt at growing them from seed was made.

By the nineteenth century, demand for imported orchids was immense, and attention turned to cultivation from seed. An entire capsule of thousands of seeds might produce

Travellers' tales

The fashion for tropical orchids in Britain started in 1732 with the Pine-pink Orchid (*Bletia purpurea*, Figs 0.1/0.1a), when Sir Charles Wager got one to flower at his home in Fulham, London. Known at the time by the synonym *Bletia verecunda*, it had been brought back from the Bahamas. Importation continued and accelerated as new species were discovered, and in 1760 the Stiff-flower Star Orchid appeared in England for the first time. The fact that these flowers were brought in from the wild was what made them so desirable, often being sold on the basis of their description alone without an accompanying sketch.

Collecting orchids became a routine part of trading activities for any ship travelling through the tropics, though this is sometimes overlooked in historical accounts due to other events taking place on the trade route. One such case is the expedition under the command of William Bligh and the ship HMS *Bounty* (Fig 0.2), mounted to take breadfruit from the tropical Pacific islands to the West Indies in order to start commercial production. This ended in failure in April 1789, when the infamous mutiny took place. However, the eminent naturalist Joseph Banks then organized another expedition, again with Bligh in charge. This returned successfully with breadfruit plants – but also with 15 orchids.

Some orchids were only discovered by chance, such as when a shipment of tropical plants was sent from Brazil to William Cattley of Barnet in London, England. Cattley, a keen orchid grower, noticed that the stout stems used as packing material were both alive and of interest. With careful cultivation he managed to grow some of this material and in November 1818 it flowered. It was not only an unknown species of orchid but also an unknown genus, with large flamboyant flowers. The leading orchid authority of the day, only a single delicate seedling and as the seedlings suffered such high mortality (for reasons then unknown), it was impossible to grow orchids from seed reliably. The only source of new orchids was from the wild, and collecting for this lucrative market was big business, leading to problems of over-collecting. In *A History of Gardening in England* (1895), Alicia Amherst wrote that orchids were packed off in their thousands, leaving their native habitats bare. Collectors of *Miltonia vexillaria* in Brazil pillaged the area that they were searching so it had "become pretty well cleared". In *Travels and Adventures of an Orchid Hunter* (1891), Albert Millican wrote that ten thousand Curled Odontoglossums were collected by cutting down four thousand trees, the camps being moved on week by week as all the plants were taken from each area.

While hothouses in Europe began to be decorated with flowering tropical orchids, the forests from which they came were being ruined. This would continue until botanists learned how to grow orchids from seed.

Figure 0.1a The Pine-pink Orchid as a modern houseplant.

Figure 0.1 The Pine-pink Orchid, the first of the tropical orchids to flower in Britain in 1732. This illustration by William Jackson Hooker, Director of the Royal Botanical Gardens, Kew, is from *Curtis's Botanical Magazine*, 1833.

Figure 0.2 A painting of HMS *Bounty* by Robert Dodd in the National Maritime Museum. It shows Captain Bligh and crew members being set adrift. The plants adorning the ship's stern are probably breadfruit.

Figure 0.4 Caricature of Sir Trevor Lawrence holding an orchid. It was illustrated by Spy (pseudonym of Sir Leslie Ward, 1851-1922) and published in *Vanity Fair* 1899.

Figure 0.3 *Cattleya labiata*.

John Lindley, described the plant in detail and named it in Cattley's honour as *Cattleya labiata*, commonly known as Cattleya (Fig. 0.3). Because nobody knew where the original 'packing' plants had been collected, the species was known only from a single plant until its rediscovery near Rio de Janeiro in 1836. By the time of the first Orchid Conference of 1885, demand for imported orchids was immense. The trade had grown from a sideline to a major part of commercial shipping, and shipments of 10,000 plants were not unknown. Sir Trevor Lawrence, then RHS President and a renowned orchid grower, commented that orchid collections were well known in Liverpool, Manchester and London, reflecting the expanding trade around all the great ports. At the same time he regretted that, due to a shortage of funds, Kew Gardens had such a small collection of plants (see Fig. 0.4).

While the fascination with orchids started out confined to hothouse species, it quickly moved towards those that were comfortable in unheated conservatories. In 1850, *Curtis's Botanical Magazine* featured *Pleione* species (Fig. 0.5) as more tolerant of cooler weather than many of the tropical orchids. It was only a matter of time before interest turned to the collection and cultivation of native orchids, the subject of this book.

Over-collecting and the Lady's Slipper Orchid: native orchids under threat

Over-collecting was not exclusive to the tropics, however. In Britain, the magnificent Lady's Slipper Orchid (Fig. 0.6), was taken close to extinction in the nineteenth century both by people picking the flowers and digging up plants for their gardens and by the destruction of its habitat in limestone woodland, which was cleared for agriculture. The Lady's Slipper Orchid was thought to be extinct until a single plant was discovered by a Mr Jarman in 1930. Its decades-long survival on the limestone of Yorkshire eventually became a conservation issue, involving some considerable discord when an enthusiast who knew the location picked the only flower for a herbarium specimen! However, seeds have since been raised artificially at Kew Gardens and the resulting plants reintroduced into the wild. By 2002, more than 300 plants were flourishing at 15 sites across northern England.

Figure 0.5 Windowsill Orchid (*Pleione formosana*). Pleiones have been out of fashion but are now very popular with growers.

Figure 0.6 The Lady's Slipper Orchid. This photograph is of a plant in Sweden.

Marsh–Common-Spotted (*Dactylorhiza*) hybrid.

The discovery of symbiotic fungi, artificial seed culture and micropropagation

In the 1890s, Noël Bernard, a French botanist who had worked on orchids during his student days, came upon a partially buried dead flower head of the Bird's-nest Orchid, which absorbs all of its nutrients from decaying organic matter in the soil. Observing that the seeds had germinated in the seed pod after apparent infection with an invasive fungus, he hypothesized that an orchid seed needs a fungal associate to ensure germination. He found that orchid seeds could be successfully germinated artificially *in vitro* using his technique of germination with symbiotic fungi. It soon became apparent that different orchids require different species of fungus, and the number of orchid species in cultivation grew rapidly with the development of Bernard's techniques.

The next major step was to discover *how* the fungus aided seed germination. In 1922, American plant physiologist Lewis Knudson found that the fungus breaks down complex sugars and starches into simple sugars, which the orchid then absorbs and utilizes for growth. Based on his research, he developed Knudsen C, a growth solution for the germination of tropical orchids. For many years this was the recipe of choice for commercial growers and it's still widely used.

While Knudsen was developing artificial seed culture, his colleague at Cornell University, Gavino Rotor, developed a technique called micropropagation, which allowed propagation of hybrid orchids. A form of micropropagation had been carried out in 1891 and 1892, when flower stalk nodes of Moth Orchids (*Phalaenopsis* species) were laid down in peat to propagate new plants. But Rotor was the first to develop true micropropagation techniques, using sterile tissue culture of sectioned flowers, which allowed a rapid increase in the generation of orchids. Now commercial growers of hybrids could generate thousands of identical plants, and make them easily available.

All of the above methods and techniques were designed for tropical orchids, but they equally apply to the hardy orchids of Northern Europe.

IN SUMMARY

Growing orchids has been a passion of gardeners for a very long time. Originally the focus was on tropical species, but attention has now turned to our exquisite native species. The experience of seeing these lovely flowers in the countryside always lifts the spirits, but they have suffered significant depletion as a result of habitat loss, so by growing them in the garden you are making an important contribution to their conservation.

Chapter One

HARDY ORCHIDS:
conservation, habitat and growing conditions

The native orchids of the British Isles are more modest-looking and compact than the exotic-looking tropical type sold in florists' shops and garden centres. They are not only superficially different in appearance, but require different habitats and growing conditions.

Opposite: Chalk Fragrant Orchid (*Gymnadenia conopsea*) with common rockrose (*Helianthemum nummularium*) and eyebright (*Euphrasia officinalis*). Limestone grassland in early July.

In the next chapter we will look at the life cycle of the native orchids of the British Isles. But for now we turn our attention to their natural habitats, to discover the growing conditions needed for successful cultivation. Once you know the requirements of individual species, which we discuss in detail in Chapter 3, you will be able to select the plants that are most likely to prosper in your soil; alternatively, with careful manipulation of the compost in containers, you will be able to grow the whole range of native orchids. The usual manuring, mulching, and so on, are not necessary: as long as our orchids have their preferred soil type and levels of sun or shade, they are not very fussy!

CONSERVATION

Orchids were once much more widespread across the whole of the British Isles than now. Some were so common that they were used to produce drinks - saloup, for example, a decoction of Early Purple Orchid root that was taken on board Captain Cook's *Endeavour* as a means of preventing scurvy.

Before modern agricultural techniques became prevalent, plants such as the Green-winged Orchid thrived. VS Summerhayes, in *Wild Orchids of Britain* (1951), says of this species: "(It) is one of the commonest of British orchids . . . not only is the species widespread, but also it sometimes occurs in immense numbers - literally in thousands or tens of thousands - so that the ground is made purple by the innumerable flower-spikes." To read Summerhayes is to rue the loss of the unimproved flower meadow: these days it is very unusual indeed to see enough orchid flowers to colour a meadow. The Green-winged Orchid was once plentiful in Derbyshire, for example, but its last site was ploughed in 1975 and there are only two records of this species in the wild since 2000.

However, despite the loss of orchid habitat in many areas, there are encouraging reports of orchids appearing in places that have been left undisturbed. Richard Mabey's *Flora Britannica* (1996) records that "Green-winged orchids made an unexpected (and unprecedented) appearance at short mid-wicket on the cricket ground at Stansted Park in West Sussex in May 1992." In Staffordshire, the creation of an artificial wildflower meadow led to Green-winged Orchids first reappearing in 1999, with many dozens flowering in 2004. A 2016 British Wildlife report on the fields of County Mayo, which are used for grazing and still unimproved, comments that "lesser butterfly orchids still turn many pastures white in June" and "marsh orchids colour road verges, pastures and shores of loughs red". These plants - past and present - were not tended or cosseted in any way; they appeared of

As long as our orchids have their preferred soil type and levels of sun or shade, they are not very fussy!

Common Spotted Orchid (*Dactylorhiza fuchsii*).

their own accord and survived the agricultural practices of the land where they grew.

These days it is hard for farmers to manage land economically and in a way that suits orchids and other wild flowers, though this is not a new problem. In *The Life of the Fields* (1884), Richard Jefferies describes how, with the coming of the railways in the late nineteenth century, there was a renaissance in dairy farming because milk could now be delivered to the big cities from deep in the countryside. Agricultural improvements were made that damaged the wild habitat – including re-sowing meadows and the careful eradication of "rattles and similar plants destructive to the hay crop".

Managing land to suit orchids is not always easy for conservation bodies either, because it requires effort and expense. A few years ago we visited a nature reserve in Somerset where the Green-winged Orchids were few and far between, as the grasses hadn't been kept down by grazing or cutting – yet there were large numbers of them just over the hedge on farmed meadowland.

Figure 1.1 Wet meadow on neutral soil with Common Spotted Orchids.

Figure 1.2 Meadow on calcareous soil with Common Spotted Orchids.

Figure 1.3 Pyramidal Orchids growing on the thin, dry soil of stabilized sand dunes.

How to grow NATIVE ORCHIDS in gardens large and small

FAVOURED HABITAT AND GROWING CONDITIONS

The orchids of Britain and Ireland favour certain habitats:

- meadows on neutral soils (Fig. 1.1)
- grassland on limestone or chalk (Fig. 1.2)
- woodland rides on moist soils and sand dunes (Fig. 1.3) (unsuitable for the garden, but we mention them only for completeness)

An orchid's preference for its habitat is determined by three key factors:

- soil conditions
- competition for light
- temperature

These factors interact, and it is the balance that determines which species will grow in a particular place.

Soil conditions

Soil conditions have the most important influence on orchid growth, with pH and levels of water and nutrients being key factors. Table 3.3 in Chapter 3 outlines the preferred conditions for the native species we recommend for cultivation.

Many of our native orchids are found growing in the more alkaline soils that overlie chalk or limestone. Such soils have low fertility because of the way that the soil chemistry works: although the mineral content of the water running through it is high, nutrients like iron, manganese and phosphorus are not readily available to plants. Orchids that prefer alkaline conditions also grow where minerals are washed out of the soil or in acid soil, where the groundwater that runs through the soil flows from limestone. So subterranean alkaline flushes of water on mountainsides that are otherwise acid heath or bog can provide a home for lime-loving orchid species.

Orchids tend to be found on the thinner soils of hill slopes, rather than the deeper soils of valley bottoms, because:

- the soil on the slopes is thinner and poorer, with a higher pH (lime content), which orchids love, compared with the richer, deeper soils in the valley;
- the lime has been washed out or diluted by the higher organic content of the valley-bottom soils;
- the slopes are at the limit of the orchid's geographical distribution and such thin soils hold less water and warm up more quickly in the spring;
- orchids do not need to compete with the more vigorous plants growing in the richer soils of the valley bottoms.

Not all of our native orchids are lime-loving. The Heath Spotted Orchid and Common Spotted Orchid are the most acid-tolerant of the native orchids and excellent candidates for growing in gardens.

Competition for light

Most of our native orchids prefer sunny conditions, though those that grow in woodland have adapted to cope with shade. Consequently, our woodland orchids can be split into two groups: shade avoiders and shade tolerators.

The Early Purple Orchid and Greater Butterfly Orchid are shade avoiders. They flower early in the year before the tree canopy is fully formed, or grow at the edges of woods and in clearings, where there is more light. Shade

Greater butterfly orchid
(*Platanthera chlorantha*).

tolerators grow in deeper shade and tend to flower later, when the tree canopy is fully expanded. Some native orchids that grow in the deepest shade have lost all of their chlorophyll (the green pigment of plants that captures the energy of sunlight). They live entirely off their fungal associate, but are unsuitable for growing in the garden. Chapter 8 gives more detail on species suitable for shady areas.

Outside woodland, native orchids will grow where there is reduced competition with more vigorous species for both light and nutrients. For example, growing on thin soils, where grazing is minimized; in meadows full of plants such as yellow rattle, which help stunt grasses; or on wet land where the lusher plants grow later in the year.

For the gardener, it's important to ensure that your orchids receive enough light to enable them both to flower *and* to produce sufficient food for the next season. If most of your garden is too shady and acid for your choice of orchid, grow them in containers (which we cover in Chapter 4). If you like to grow spring- or early-summer-flowering orchids, extend the flowering display by mixed plantings with later-flowering plants, but don't let them overtop or crowd out the orchids until these have flowered and begun to wither. Chapters 4, 7, 8 and 9 include ideas for suitable plants to combine with orchids in your garden.

Temperature

The temperature range for orchids is quite large. Higher temperatures are tolerated, as long as adequate water is available. If there is a drought, though, a high temperature will severely harm the plant as water loss increases. On the other hand, when the orchids are dormant in winter, less water is better as this reduces the problems of root rot that can occur at low temperatures. As most of our native orchids are winter dormant, we will return to the distinction between them and winter-green species in Chapter 2.

IN SUMMARY

Once established, our native orchids are robust plants and a delight to grow. While getting them started can be a challenge, it is well worth it for the sheer joy of success. The trick is to get them established so that they can thrive and become a special part of your garden flora.

If you reproduce the agricultural practices of yesteryear on a small scale in your garden, and select the right orchids, you will be recreating a slice of the once-magnificent 'natural' gardens our grandparents would have known.

Chapter Two

The structure and life cycle of native ORCHIDS

When looking at an orchid flower, it's difficult to see how its seemingly complex structure could come about - and why. Understanding this structure and the life cycle of the plant helps explain why orchids have to be cultivated in a special way to ensure they can establish in your garden. In this chapter we explore the intricacies of our native orchids' biology.

Opposite: Early Marsh Orchid (*Dactylorhiza incarnata*) with creeping willow (*Salix repens*), marsh bedstraw (*Galium palustre*) and dewberry (*Rubus caesius*). Dune slack in mid-June.

THE STRUCTURE OF AN ORCHID FLOWER

Orchids are monocotyledons or monocots: flowering plants that germinate with a single seed leaf (cotyledon). They are perennials that grow from a fleshy root or tuber, and their flowers have a distinguishable shape that is consistent among all orchid species. (Monocots are the smaller group of the two categories of flowering plants, dicotyledons and monocotyledons. They typically have long, stalkless leaves, e.g. grasses, lilies, palms and orchids have their own family, *Orchidaceae*, within this group.)

Although the native orchids of the British Isles have flower spikes made up of small flowers, the individual flowers are essentially the same as those of the large single flowers of tropical species. Take a close look at a flower on a wild orchid to see how they really are no different, biologically, from the blowsy tropical versions. They are just smaller.

The prominent parts of the orchid flower are the three petals and the three sepals, which start life as covers for the flower bud. Each set of three is placed roughly equidistantly in a whorl, and the two whorls are offset by about 60 degrees. If the petals and sepals were all the same shape, the flower would look like a six-pointed star. In most orchids, when the flower opens, the top point of the star is a sepal (the upper sepal) and the bottom point of the star is a petal (the lip). The other sepals and petals are the points at the two sides of the star, one of each on each side (the lateral sepals and lateral petals). This structure is illustrated in Figures 2.1 and 2.2.

Sun Orchids, from the southern hemisphere, have such star-shaped flowers, but most orchids, including our native species, have

Figure 2.1 The flower of a tropical Slipper Orchid. LP: lateral petal. LS: lateral sepal. US: upper sepal. L: lip. C: column.

modified sepals or petals or both, so the flowers are bilaterally symmetrical and the star-shaped structure is not always obvious.

In the tropical Slipper Orchids (Fig. 2.1), the lateral sepals are reduced and fused into one structure, the upper sepal is hugely expanded and embellished, and the lip is curled upwards to form a large pitcher.

Figure 2.2 shows three examples of British and Irish native orchid flowers. In the Common Spotted Orchid, the upper sepal and lateral petals are formed into a hood; the Bee Orchid has a large balloon-shaped lip, and the lateral petals are reduced to short tubular structures; the lip of the Marsh Helleborine is divided into two parts – a 'landing stage' at the front (the epichile) and a cup for nectar at the back (the hypochile).

Unique to orchids is the column, which is a fusion of the structures that carry the pollen-producing cells and the pollen-receiving cells. After pollination, the seeds are produced

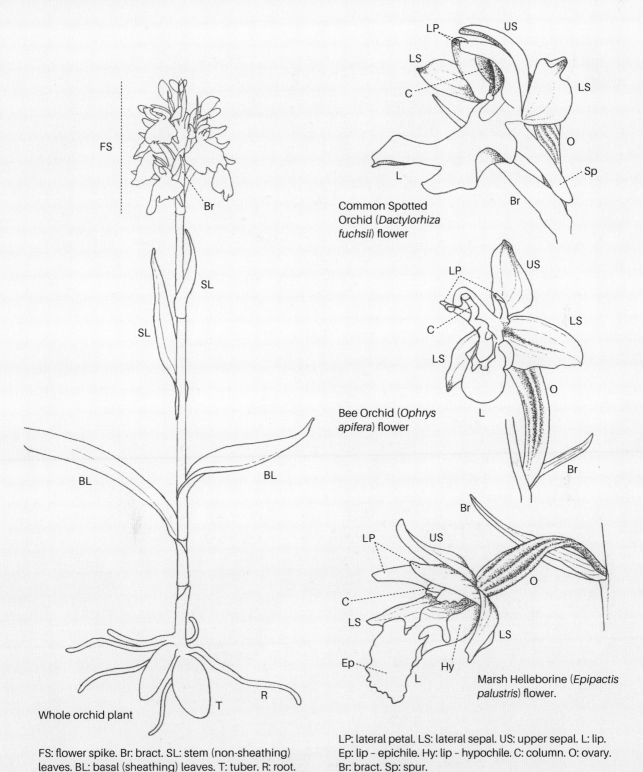

Common Spotted Orchid (*Dactylorhiza fuchsii*) flower

Bee Orchid (*Ophrys apifera*) flower

Marsh Helleborine (*Epipactis palustris*) flower.

Whole orchid plant

FS: flower spike. Br: bract. SL: stem (non-sheathing) leaves. BL: basal (sheathing) leaves. T: tuber. R: root.

LP: lateral petal. LS: lateral sepal. US: upper sepal. L: lip. Ep: lip – epichile. Hy: lip – hypochile. C: column. O: ovary. Br: bract. Sp: spur.

Figure 2.2 The structure and features of an orchid.

The structure and life cycle of native ORCHIDS

Early Marsh Orchid (*Dactylorhiza incarnata*).

in the ovary, situated at the back of the flower, where there is sometimes a spur - a hollow organ with nectar at the very bottom to entice long-tongued pollinators.

All orchid flowers - whether on a single stem in a tropical rainforest or on a flower spike in a British meadow - rotate on their flower stalks before opening; in most cases through 180 degrees. This brings the flower the right way up for the function it is to serve, placing the lip at the bottom as a 'landing stage' for pollinators, with the column above. If you look at the flower stalk of an orchid, you should be able to see the twist. This is clearly shown in the loose flower spike of the Greater Butterfly Orchid (Fig. 2.3). The Bog Orchid has a stalk rotation of a full 360 degrees, bringing the flower back to its original orientation, but the advantage of this curious flower rotation remains unknown.

All these features of the orchid flower are associated with attracting pollinating insects, and often it is a unique association - one orchid species with one insect - that has resulted in the vast range of orchid flower shapes. They are designed so that the insect can only approach from one direction. At the same time the 'face' of the orchid is often so developed that it looks like a specific insect, usually a bee or wasp species, so that it attracts males into thinking it is a female mate. This effect is sometimes compounded by the orchid producing a scent that is a very close analogue of the attraction pheromone for that specific insect.

THE IDIOSYNCRASIES OF ORCHID SEED

Unlike the seeds of tropical orchids, which germinate in light, seeds of orchids native to Northern Europe will only germinate in darkness. All orchid seeds are very small - the smallest seeds in the world. Quite how minute they are can be seen in Figures 2.4 to 2.6. The seed is like dust - and, like dust, it is easily blown in the wind. To achieve this small size, the endosperm - the food-containing tissue within a seed, normally full of starch - is absent; and the embryo is tiny - only a small ball of cells, accompanied by some oil droplets and starch grains. If you break open a ripe orchid seed capsule on a still day, the seeds fall out looking like a wisp of smoke, but they fall to earth within a few feet. On a windy day they disappear into the distance, to settle when the wind drops or the rain washes them out of the air.

Orchid seeds also all exhibit a very specific pattern of construction, visible in Figures 2.4 and 2.5. Only the practised eye can separate orchid seeds into different groups and identify an orchid with any confidence from its seed alone.

Figure 2.3 The Greater Butterfly Orchid in profile, showing the twist in the flower stalk and the long spur at the back of the flower, which contains nectar at the end for pollinating moths.

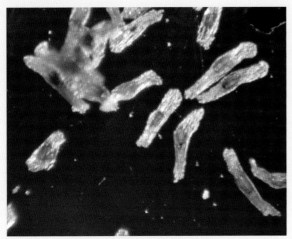

Figure 2.4 Green-winged Orchid seeds.

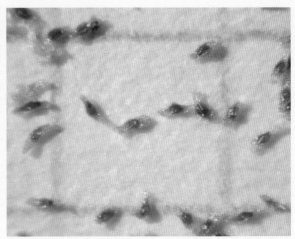

Figure 2.5 Orchid seeds on graph paper: each square is 2mm across.

Figure 2.6 Green-winged Orchid seeds next to a grape pip, for scale.

Figure 2.7 The Green-winged Orchid. Remarkable that such tiny seeds can grow into a sturdy plant like this.

Although seed production is enormous, the tiny seeds have no energy reserves on which to call. In this they differ from the seed of virtually every other plant, which can rely on their food reserves until they produce leaves and start to photosynthesize. As we saw in Chapter 1, what orchids need in nature is a symbiotic fungus to provide them with essential nutrients while they get started. Many plants have symbiotic fungal associations, helping with the uptake of phosphates and nitrogen, but these fungal associates are more fundamental for orchids. They provide the energy the plant needs in the form of sugars, which are essential for growth in the first stages of the plant's life, and it can take years before an orchid produces its first leaf and starts to actively photosynthesize. When orchids are germinated in artificial conditions, however, a special growth medium can take the place of this symbiotic fungus and provide all the necessary nutrients.

With this slow rate of growth and the threats that a plant must survive before it gets to flowering size, it is no wonder that even common orchid species are not common except in local colonies – and that they cope with the challenges of germination by producing huge amounts of seed. For example, a well-grown Common Spotted Orchid produces half a million seeds every year, so that a handful will find the right conditions to grow.

What this means for the gardener

Our native orchids have a long life. In perfect conditions, some species take only a month to germinate, while others will take six months to a year before they start to produce a shoot or root, before spending one or two years underground.

The Common Spotted Orchid generally

> *What orchids need in nature is a symbiotic fungus to provide them with essential nutrients while they get started.*

produces its first leaves one to two years from germination and it is another year before the leaves are developed enough for the plant to produce flowers. The Early Purple Orchid will often take two years to produce leaves. Other species involve even longer time scales: the Bee Orchid, Pyramidal Orchid and Broad-leaved Helleborine may take six to eight years to flower. Orchids grown in sterile and perfect conditions, however, will take considerably less time.

It is this long development process that makes it so destructive to dig up a flowering orchid plant. Being slow to establish, dependent on their fungal associations, and vulnerable to root damage when disturbed, an uprooted orchid will not survive the move. So, if you hope to grow orchids in your garden, buy well-grown plants from a reputable supplier (see Resources), who will have raised them in a suitable medium with minimal root disturbance. Bought-in plants will have the equivalent of several years' natural growth behind them and be

Figure 2.8 Southern Marsh Orchids established in a garden meadow may take patience to develop to this point, but it is well worth the effort.

only a season away from flowering. Once established in your garden, they will look after themselves. Some will naturally produce clumps of flowers and most will eventually set seed and produce new plants (Fig 2.8).

Growing orchids from seed in a chemical medium is covered in detail in Chapter 5.

THE FUNGAL PARTNER

As we have seen, an orchid is dependent upon its fungal partner until it grows large enough to produce green leaves. However, this relationship is complex, and there is evidence that when the orchid is green and photosynthesizing, the fungus can in turn receive food from the plant.

Some orchid species appear to require a specific fungus, while others are more easy-going. But their fungal dependency is why an orchid species may die out from, or fail to colonize, an apparently suitable site: because the necessary fungus has encountered a problem like an attack by another pathogenic fungus. A few of the less common species in Northern Europe have a strange distribution, where they appear in relatively large numbers in a few places but do not grow at all in similar habitats. This is true of the Burnt Orchid, whose fungal partner's erratic distribution may explain this.

Certain orchids switch fungal partners during their life, with different partners when they are young and subterranean, when they are older and green, or when something significant changes in their environment. The orchid is the master in the relationship, however, as the fungus is kept to the surface tissue and is picked up or discarded as required.

GERMINATION AND EARLY GROWTH BELOW GROUND

Orchids remain underground during the first stage of their life. Figure 2.9 shows the development cycle at this stage. It starts with the seed, which is a simple structure, with just an outer covering (the testa) enclosing an air space and the embryo.

Since there is no food in the seed, it needs to land close to its prospective fungal partner in order to germinate or survive once it has germinated. Next, hyphae (the branching filaments of a fungus) grow into the orchid cell, where they form coil-like structures called pelotons, which are digested by the orchid cell. The cell is not damaged in any way, and new pelotons can be formed by hyphae growing back into the cell.

As the orchid embryo grows, it becomes organized into a more recognizable tissue structure shaped like a small tuber, called the protocorm. Now the fungal partner is restricted

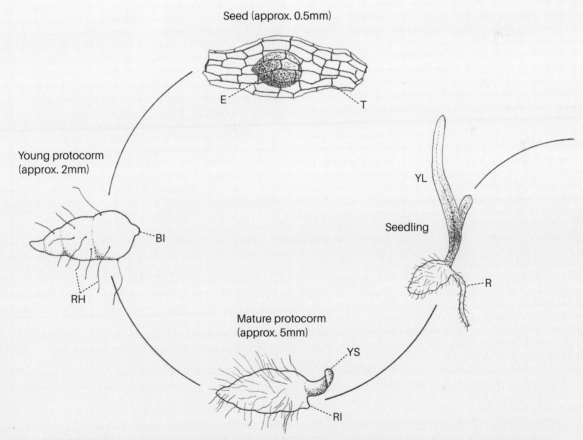

Seed (approx. 0.5mm)

Young protocorm (approx. 2mm)

YL

Seedling

BI

R

RH

Mature protocorm (approx. 5mm)

YS

RI

Figure 2.9 The development of an orchid from seed to young seedling. E: embryo. T: testa. BI: bud initial. RH: root hairs. YS: young shoot. RI: root initial. YL: young leaf. R: root.

to the outer layers, and the protocorm develops root hairs and a 'bud initial'. Once the protocorm has harvested enough food from the fungal partner, the bud initial will begin to grow into a young shoot, and a 'root initial' will form and grow into a root. Only when the young shoot breaks through the soil surface and emerges into the light will it start to produce young leaves.

THE GREEN PLANT

Once the seedling has emerged above ground, it needs a further period of vegetative growth, producing more leaves and a tuber or rhizome (see page 42 ['Rhizome types and winter-dormant types']), before it will flower.

In Common Spotted Orchids and Southern Marsh Orchids, there is always at least one year of vegetative growth, but they usually flower in the third year after germinating and then every year for many years. The first Southern Marsh Orchid in our meadows flowered for more than a decade.

Usually the first green leaf appears when the root system is still very small, and it may be the only leaf that grows. In the second year there are four or five leaves, and the overwintering 'resting bud' (Fig. 2.11) is really quite fat, with an extensive root system. When the bud is fat like this, you can be sure that the orchid will flower in the next season. Figures 2.10-2.13 show the progress of a Common Spotted Orchid germinated in culture, which is described in Chapter 5. At a year old it was taken out of culture. At this point it had a single leaf. Then, in early spring the following year, it was potted on into the three-inch pot shown in the photographs. By July of that year, more or less the end of the growing season, it had become a sizeable plant (Fig. 2.10) and by the winter the

Figure 2.10 A two-year-old Common Spotted Orchid that had been germinated and grown in culture for the first ten months of its life.

Figure 2.11 The resting bud of the same Common Spotted Orchid at two and a half years old.

rootball filled the pot (Fig. 2.12). From the size of the resting bud (Fig. 2.11) and its early growth (Fig. 2.13) the next year, it was clear that it would flower, which it did in June (Figs 2.14 and 2.15), three years after germination.

The adult flowering plant will typically have a number of large basal leaves that sheath the stem, some leaves higher up the stem that are not sheathing, and leaf-like structures called bracts, which extend under the flowers in the flower spike (see Figure 2.2, page 33).

Figure 2.12 The overwintering root system of the same Common Spotted Orchid at two and a half years old.

Figure 2.13 Early spring growth of the same Common Spotted Orchid at two years and nine months.

Figure 2.14 The same Common Spotted Orchid, now in flower at three years old.

THE BELOW-GROUND STRUCTURE AND ANNUAL GROWTH CYCLE

All orchids are perennials, and the best native orchids to grow in gardens flower for more than a year, often for many years, before dying.

Although some species are said to flower once and then die, this is not inevitable (see page 45 ['Year-round growth and care']). How the adult plant survives from year to year varies between orchid species, there being three basic types of overwintering strategy: underground as a rhizome; underground as a tuber; or above ground

The structure and life cycle of native ORCHIDS

Figure 2.15 Close-up of the same orchid in flower at three years old.

as a rosette of green leaves, with a strong tuberous root system anchoring them down against the vagaries of winter wind and rain. So gardeners should avoid digging over the plot, as patience is likely to be rewarded with new growth.

A great many tropical orchids and some of our native orchids use a fourth method for storage while resting, and that is a swollen stem that sits just above the soil surface, called a pseudobulb. Only a couple of rare British orchids have pseudobulbs, but a number of the foreign hardy orchids grown in our gardens are of this type.

Rhizome types

The rhizome is an underground stem that grows horizontally like a root. Helleborines are typical of this growth pattern. Food is stored in the rhizome, and if enough has been accumulated during the previous growing season, a 'resting bud' at the tip of the rhizome will start growing in the spring and turn upwards to form a leafy shoot. New buds are formed at the base of the upright shoot, which will grow out to form a new rhizome. The current season's leafy growth will wither and die by the autumn, and the plant survives the winter as the underground rhizome. The amount of branching, speed of rhizome growth, and thickness of the rhizome varies between species. In the Broad-leaved Helleborine, for example, the rhizome is thick, slow-growing and seldom branches, while the rhizome in the Marsh Helleborine is thin, fast-growing and often branches.

Winter-dormant and winter-green tuber types

A root tuber, finger-shaped or oval, is the more common food-storage structure among native orchids of the British Isles. When the above-ground leafy shoot withers away, it leaves a resting bud more or less at the soil surface, with the root tuber immediately below. In some species, such as the Southern Marsh Orchid and Common Spotted Orchid, the rest period is in winter, hence they are 'winter dormant'. In others – the Bee Orchid, for example – the rest period is in late summer, and by autumn its bud has broken and the plant spends the winter with a rosette of basal leaves lying on, or very close to, the ground. This type of orchid is called 'winter green'. Each year the orchid plant grows up using the food from the tuber it surmounts, and during the growing season a new tuber develops ready for next year's plant. Figure 2.16 shows this annual growth cycle for an orchid with a tuber.

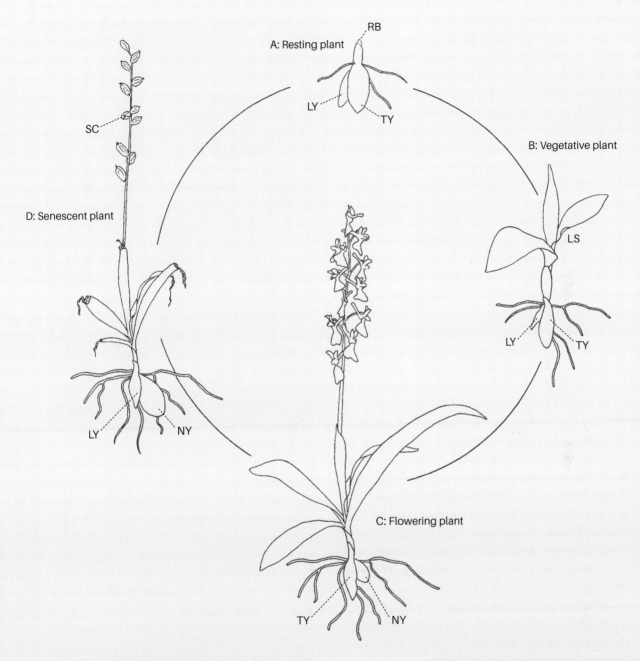

Figure 2.16 The annual growth cycle of an orchid with a tuber. TY: this year's tuber. LY: last year's tuber. NY: next year's tuber. RB: resting bud. LS: leafy shoot. SC: seed capsules.

For winter-dormant species, (A) is winter, (B) is spring, (C) is early summer and (D) is late summer/autumn. For winter-green species, (A) is late summer/early autumn, (B) is over winter and into spring, (C) is early summer and (D) is late summer.

Species whose storage structure is a rhizome have the same cycle except that instead of a new tuber developing during (B) to (D), a new section of rhizome grows, with next year's shoot bud developing at the end of the new rhizome section between (D) and (A).

At this time of year the heat of the summer sun dries everything up and the countryside rests until the autumn rains reappear.

Figure 2.17 A natural clump of Common Spotted Orchids growing in a sand-dune habitat.

It is likely that winter-green species have their stronghold in the Mediterranean, where they grow when the soil is wet from late autumn and then continue growing through an early flowering season, followed by a dormant phase in late summer. At this time of year the heat of the summer sun dries everything up and the countryside rests until the autumn rains reappear. But whether a plant rests in the late summer or over winter, the growth pattern is the same.

Winter-green species in the British Isles are broadly divided into two: those of the genus *Ophrys* and those of the genus *Anacamptis*. The *Ophrys* genus has many different species, though they are all so close in structure that they are not always easy to distinguish by eye without practice. The one most easily recognized and that can be cultivated in the garden is the Bee Orchid (*O. apifera*). In the *Anacamptis*

genus there is the Pyramidal Orchid (*A. pyramidalis*) and the Green-winged Orchid (*A. morio*).

Orchids that form clumps

The orchids whose resting structures are modified stems, i.e. rhizomes and pseudobulbs, are more likely to branch and form clumps than those with root tubers.

Sometimes orchids with root tubers will produce extra buds and divide naturally to produce clumps, which are very striking when they do (Figs 2.17 and 2.18), but this is unusual and none of the orchids in our meadows have ever done so.

Figure 2.18 A natural clump of Early Purple Orchids growing along a woodland ride.

Year-round growth and care

Since all of our native orchids retain a fungal association throughout their life, it is possible that if the growing season has been hard for them and they have not been able to accumulate enough resources to produce a green shoot and flower in the next season, they can stay underground and build up resources by living off the fungus. This is quite normal for many species. So don't despair if your orchid does not reappear one year – it won't necessarily have died.

As we now know, orchids really do not like disturbance, so if your orchids are in ground that you cultivate, mark their position so that you can safely work around them in the autumn and winter. Even hoeing is to be avoided.

IN SUMMARY

The structure and growth pattern of our native orchids is truly extraordinary; something to be marvelled at. Although the life cycle is complicated and the survival of plants may seem unlikely, a few well-chosen plants from a reputable supplier, together with a little care and patience, should reward you with a beautiful and long-term garden population.

In the next chapter we look at how to choose species that are suitable for conditions in your garden.

Chapter Three

Native
ORCHIDS
suitable for
cultivation

There are about 50 British and Irish native orchids. The number is imprecise because botanists are continually reviewing them in light of new DNA evidence. Also, some extremely rare species may have become extinct, but we cannot be sure because they are so rare and because orchids can spend extended periods living below ground. Then there are new arrivals from the Continent, perhaps as a result of global warming. Finally, certain groups, in particular the Marsh Orchids, hybridize quite readily, producing beautiful plants that may eventually be classed as new species.

Opposite: Pyramidal Orchid (*Anacamptis pyramidalis*) with common restharrow (*Ononis repens*) and kidney vetch (*Anthyllis vulneraria*). Dune slack in late June.

In this chapter we describe the 14 species that we think are best suited to growing in gardens. We have experience of growing most of these ourselves and find that with the right degree of care and attention, they are not difficult. They are the more common of our native orchids and are all rather beautiful. We also summarize a further 12 species that you might like to try your hand at. These are listed separately because either they are more difficult to grow or they may be less interesting to gardeners due to their small size or plain appearance.

The species we have excluded from either list all have a 'threatened' conservation status, meaning that they are rare and at risk of being lost from our native flora. They will often have some special requirement, which means that the chance of success in the garden is very small and collecting seed will only further endanger the species. Table 3.1 shows a full list of the British and Irish native species and their conservation status.

The overview of recommended species is divided into two sections. The first describes those that require sunny conditions; the second, those that will grow in shade. To help you decide on a planting scheme for your particular situation, Table 3.2 (page 51) summarizes the characteristics of these species, while Table 3.3 (page 52) shows the growing conditions they prefer and the situations where they are found in the wild. Tables 3.4 and 3.5 (pages 64 and 71) summarize the characteristics and growing conditions of the 11 other possible species you may like to try growing.

TABLE 3.1. BRITISH AND IRISH NATIVE ORCHID SPECIES			
Common name	**Latin name**	**Schedule 8***	**Red List category****
Recommended species for cultivation			
Bee Orchid	*Ophrys apifera*		LC
Broad-leaved Helleborine	*Epipactis helleborine*		LC
Chalk Fragrant Orchid	*Gymnadenia conopsea*		LC
Common Spotted Orchid	*Dactylorhiza fuchsii*		LC
Common Twayblade	*Neottia ovata*		LC
Early Marsh Orchid	*Dactylorhiza incarnata*		LC
Early Purple Orchid	*Orchis mascula*		LC
Greater Butterfly Orchid	*Platanthera chlorantha*		NT
Green-winged Orchid	*Anacamptis morio*		NT
Heath Spotted Orchid	*Dactylorhiza maculata*		LC
Marsh Helleborine	*Epipactis palustris*		LC
Northern Marsh Orchid	*Dactylorhiza purpurella*		LC

See page 50 for footnotes to Table 3.1.

Pyramidal Orchid	*Anacamptis pyramidalis*		LC
Southern Marsh Orchid	*Dactylorhiza praetermissa*		LC
Other possible species for cultivation			
Autumn Lady's-tresses	*Spiranthes spiralis*		NT
Bird's-nest Orchid***	*Neottia nidus-avis*		NT
Bog Orchid	*Hammarbya paludosa*		LC
Creeping Lady's-tresses	*Goodyera repens*		LC
Dark-red Helleborine	*Epipactis atrorubens*		LC (NS)
Dense-flowered Orchid	*Neotinea maculata*		NT
Green-flowered Helleborine	*Epipactis phyllanthes*		LC (NS)
Heath Fragrant Orchid	*Gymnadenia borealis*		LC
Irish Lady's-tresses	*Spiranthes romanzoffiana*		LC (NS)
Lesser Twayblade	*Listera cordata*		LC
Narrow-leaved Marsh Orchid	*Dactylorhiza traunsteineri*		LC (NS)
Violet Helleborine	*Epipactis purpurata*		LC
Threatened species (not recommended)			
Burnt Orchid	*Orchis ustulata*		EN
Coralroot Orchid	*Corallorhiza trifida*		VU
Dune Helleborine	*Epipactis dunensis*		DD (NR)
Early Spider Orchid	*Ophrys sphegodes*	Yes	LC (NS)
Fen Orchid	*Liparis loeselii*	Yes	EN
Fly Orchid	*Ophrys insectifera*		VU
Frog Orchid	*Coeloglossum viride*		VU
Ghost Orchid	*Epipogium aphyllum*	Yes	EX
Greater Tongue Orchid	*Serapias lingua*		DD
Hebridean Marsh Orchid	*Dactylorhiza ebudensis*		VU
Irish Marsh Orchid	*Dactylorhiza occidentalis*		DD
Lady Orchid	*Orchis purpurea*		EN
Lady's Slipper Orchid	*Cypripedium calceolus*	Yes	CR

See page 50 for footnotes to Table 3.1.

Lapland Marsh Orchid	*Dactylorhiza traunsteinerioides* subsp. *Lapponica*	Yes	DD
Late Spider Orchid	*Ophrys fuciflora*	Yes	VU
Lesser Butterfly Orchid	*Platanthera bifolia*		VU
Lizard Orchid	*Himantoglossum hircinum*	Yes	NT
Loose-flowered Orchid	*Orchis laxiflora*		DD
Man Orchid	*Aceras anthropophorum*		EN
Marsh Fragrant Orchid	*Gymnadenia densiflora*		DD
Military Orchid	*Orchis militaris*	Yes	VU
Monkey Orchid	*Orchis simia*	Yes	VU
Musk Orchid	*Herminium monorchis*		VU
Narrow-lipped Helleborine	*Epipactis leptochila*		DD (NS)
Red Helleborine	*Cephalanthera rubra*	Yes	CR
Small White Orchid	*Pseudorchis albida*		VU
Small-flowered Tongue Orchid	*Serapias parviflora*		(NR)
Summer Lady's-tresses	*Spiranthes aestivalis*		EX
Sword-leaved Helleborine	*Cephalanthera longifolia*		VU
White Helleborine	*Cephalanthera damasonium*		VU
Young's Helleborine	*Epipactis youngiana*	Yes	DD

* Schedule 8 of the Wildlife and Countryside act 1981 (see Chapter 5) is a list of rare and protected species which by law must not be touched, which includes collecting the seeds.

** The Red List of Threatened Species, produced by the IUCN (International Union for the Conservation of Nature), is a comprehensive inventory of the global conservation status of biological species. The Red List categories and their acronyms used here are as follows:

Lower-risk status: LC = least concern; NT= near-threatened.

Threatened status: VU = vulnerable; EN = endangered; CR = critical.

Other: DD = data deficient; EX = extinct.

Not all species have a Red List category, because in some cases there is insufficient data to make the assessment, but since this almost by definition means that they are rare, we have included these in the 'Threatened' section of this table. In some cases we have also included information from the Scarce Atlas (a project undertaken by the Botanical Society of Britain and Ireland, the Biological Records Centre and the Joint Nature Conservation Committee) as a further indication of status. These are shown in brackets: (NS) = nationally scarce; (NR) = nationally rare.

*** The bird's-nest orchid is included with the group of other possible species for cultivation in this table because of its conservation status, but we have not included it in Table 3.5 because it is a saprophytic plant that relies solely on a fungal associate to survive, and as such would be a very great challenge for any gardener.

TABLE 3.2. RECOMMENDED SPECIES' CHARACTERISTICS

Species	Height when in flower (cm)*	Flowering time**	Flower spike			Sheathing leaves		Storage organ	Winter green	Fragrant
			Length (cm)	Colour	Appearance	Shape	Spotted			
Bee Orchid	15-45	June	3-12	Pink and brown	Very loose	Oblong		Tuber	Yes	
Broad-leaved helleborine	25-80	Late July to mid-August	7-30	Greenish to reddish	Long and very loose	Oval		Rhizome		
Chalk Fragrant Orchid	15-40	Mid-June to mid-July	6-10	Pink-red lilac	Quite dense cylinder	Strap		Tuber		Yes
Common Spotted Orchid	15-50	June to July	3.5-12.5	Rose-pink to white	Cylindrical	Strap	Yes	Tuber		
Common Twayblade	20-60	Mid-May to early August	7-25	Green	Narrow cylinder	Oval		Rhizome		
Early Marsh Orchid	15-50	Late May and June	2.5-10	Pale yellow to bright magenta	Rather dense cylinder	Strap		Tuber		
Early Purple Orchid	15-60	Early April to early June	4-15	Purple	Loose cylinder	Strap	Yes	Tuber		
Greater Butterfly Orchid	20-40	Late May to late July	5-20	White with green tinge	Loose cylinder	Oval		Tuber		Yes
Green-winged Orchid	10-40	May	2.5-8	Red-purple to lilac	Loose cylinder	Oblong		Tuber	Yes	
Heath Spotted Orchid	15-50	June to July	2.5-10.5	Pale pink to white	Rounded	Strap	Usually	Tuber		
Marsh Helleborine	15-45	July	7-15	Purplish-brown and white	Loose, one-sided cylinder	Broad strap		Rhizome		
Northern Marsh Orchid	10-25	June to mid-July	2.5-7.5	Deep purple or magenta	Rather dense broad cylinder	Broad strap	Usually not	Tuber		
Pyramidal Orchid	20-50	Mid-June to end July	2-5	Rosy purple	Dense, conical	Strap		Tuber	Yes	
Southern Marsh Orchid	15-60	late May to early July	5-15	Reddish-lilac	Cylindrical	Strap		Tuber		

* This shows the normal range in flowering height. Robust plants growing in good conditions can often be taller and, similarly, plants growing under stress can be smaller.
** This is the main flowering period. Flowering often starts earlier in the southern or lower-altitude reaches of the species' range and finishes later in the northern or higher reaches.

TABLE 3.3. RECOMMENDED SPECIES' TYPICAL GROWING CONDITIONS

	Soil conditions	Plant community
Bee Orchid	Poor, well-drained soils. Prefers calcareous soils but will grow on neutral-to-slightly-acid soils.	Typically open grassland with a short sward.
Broad-leaved Helleborine	Calcareous to slightly acid soils with average moisture.	Deciduous woodland, wood margins, hedgerows.
Chalk Fragrant Orchid	Dry calcareous soils.	Grassland with a long or short sward.
Common Spotted Orchid	Typically damp neutral soils but tolerates a broad range, from calcareous to slightly acid, and dry to wet.	Tall and short grassland, amongst scrub and open areas of woodland.
Common Twayblade	Prefers calcareous but wide-ranging, even to slightly acid soils.	Grassland, pastures, scrub, hedgerows and open woodland.
Early Marsh Orchid	Wet or moist, often peaty, soils; calcareous to slightly acid.	Wet meadows, marshes, bogs, fens and dune slacks.
Early Purple Orchid	Prefers calcareous soils which are dry to moist but not wet. Avoids acid soils.	Woods and copses, but not deep shade, and open pastures.
Greater Butterfly Orchid	Dry to moist calcareous soils.	Woods and grassy slopes.
Green-winged Orchid	Neutral or calcareous soils, with some preference for the latter; damp but not wet.	Meadows and pastures with short sward. Never in woods.
Heath Spotted Orchid	Moist acid, sometimes neutral, peaty soils; not too boggy nor too dry.	Heathland, moorland, meadows and hill pastures.
Marsh Helleborine	Wet calcareous-to-neutral soils.	Fens and dune slacks; sometimes wet grazed meadows.
Northern Marsh Orchid	Wet or moist soils, calcareous to slightly acid.	Marshes, fens, damp pastures and dune slacks.
Pyramidal Orchid	Dry calcareous soils.	Grassland, usually in a long sward, and amongst scrub.
Southern Marsh Orchid	Wet or moist calcareous-to-neutral soils, often peaty.	Damp meadows, water meadows, lowland peat bogs, fens, marshes and dune slacks.

SPECIES SUITABLE FOR SUNNY SITUATIONS

These orchid species are typically found growing in open situations in the wild, so will certainly be suitable for sunny conditions in the garden. They are listed here broadly in order of their preference for soil moisture, from drier conditions to wetter soils. This is not a precise ordering, because several have a wide range of tolerances and for some – the Marsh Orchids, for example – there is no practical difference between the species in this respect.

Bee Orchid
(*Ophrys apifera*)

Of all of our native orchids, the Bee Orchid epitomizes the exotic reputation of the orchid family, and most people are truly thrilled and fascinated when they first see it. The flower's lip looks like a brown, furry bee and has three triangular pink sepals radiating from it, giving the effect of a bee sitting on a flower (Fig. 3.1). This mimicry is designed to facilitate cross-pollination. It fools passing male bees into believing the lip is a female bee, so they try to mate with it and end up collecting or depositing pollen.

Figure 3.1 Bee Orchid. The lip looks just like a bee visiting a pink flower.

The Bee Orchid is winter-green (see Chapter 2, page 42), its leaves growing in the autumn and spending the winter as a basal rosette. The stem starts growing in mid- to late spring, and the flowers open between late May and early July, depending on location, but most flowering occurs in June. Bee Orchid numbers can fluctuate markedly from year to year, even though we now know the adult plant is quite long-lived. (It was once thought to be monocarpic, i.e. flowering once and then dying.) This fluctuation likely results from a depletion of resources when flowering, forcing the plant to spend a year or two below ground, or as a non-flowering rosette, while it restocks its energy supplies.

The Bee Orchid is something of a colonizer. It often appears on recently disturbed sites on a variety of soils, but is then lost as more competitive plants move in. It does persist indefinitely at sites that are undisturbed, in particular open grassland, especially if the soil is calcareous (alkaline) and not too wet. It is widely distributed in England, Wales and Ireland, but is most frequent in the south and east of England.

If you can offer the Bee Orchid a home in a well-drained soil of low fertility and in a reasonably open situation, you can look forward to enjoying this iconic species in your garden for years to come.

Pyramidal Orchid
(*Anacamptis pyramidalis*)

The Pyramidal Orchid is named for the shape of its flower spike, which has a triangular profile when the flowers first begin to open (Fig. 3.2). The 50 or so flowers are tightly packed in the spike and they open from the bottom upwards. In bud they are a dark cerise, verging on purple, while the open flower is a paler cerise, so the opening spike appears to be two-tone. Once all the flowers are open, the spike is globe shaped. Occasionally white-flowered forms of the species appear.

This is another winter-green species. Its stem starts to grow in spring and the plant usually flowers between mid-June and mid-July.

The Pyramidal Orchid has a mostly southerly distribution in Britain and Ireland,

Figure 3.2 A Pyramidal Orchid that has just started to flower, showing the two-tone pyramidal spike.

Green-winged Orchid
(*Anacamptis morio*)

One of our most beautiful orchids and once one of the commonest, in times gone by the Green-winged Orchid brought an uplifting purple haze to pastures when it flowered en masse in the late spring.

In this orchid the lateral sepals are held directly forwards, displaying the prominent dark veins which are often dark green (Fig. 3.3), hence the plant's name - Green-winged or Green-veined Orchid. The base colour of the flower is usually a deep purple, but large groups often have plenty of variation, with

but does occur all the way up to Scotland, though it tends to become restricted to the coast in the northerly parts of its range. It prefers grassland where there is some lime in the soil. It is also one of the first species to appear in highly disturbed, artificial habitats, often emerging on new road embankments.

Pyramidals grow well in grass with a longer sward, partly because of the head start they get in the growing season from being green during winter and early spring. On the other hand, their restriction to milder coastal areas in the north suggests they are susceptible to frost. We recommend growing Pyramidals in a free-draining soil so they don't become too wet over winter, and in locations where they are protected from severe frosts.

Figure 3.3 Green-winged Orchid. The lateral sepals have prominent dark veins.

paler purple, rosy-pink or sometimes white-flowered specimens.

The Green-winged is a winter-green plant. Even at flowering time, this orchid is a diminutive plant that needs a short sward to show it at its best. Like the Bee Orchid, it was once thought to be monocarpic because of its fluctuating numbers between flowering seasons, but it is now known to be quite as long-lasting as the Bee and Fragrant Orchids.

The distribution of the Green-winged Orchid almost exactly matches that of the Bee Orchid: that is, widespread in England, Wales and Ireland and absent from Scotland. It prefers calcareous soils but will happily grow on neutral clayey soils that are not too wet. It requires a short turf and the non-shady conditions found, for example, in old pastures, meadows and calcareous downland, or any habitat that mimics these conditions. It characteristically grows with cowslips, and this combination can make for a wonderful garden lawn during spring and early summer.

Chalk Fragrant Orchid
(*Gymnadenia conopsea*)

The three Fragrant Orchids are now treated as distinct species. They are all very similar, and the best way of separating them, though by no means foolproof, is by the habitat they are growing in. The Chalk Fragrant, also known as the Common Fragrant Orchid, is the one we think is best suited to the garden. It is a plant of chalk or limestone grassland. We also include the Heath Fragrant Orchid as another possible species to grow. It is more tolerant of low-pH soils and may be found on hill pastures with acid soils or with heather and grasses on moorland. For more on this, see Table 3.4 on page 64.

The Chalk Fragrant is an exquisite orchid (Fig. 3.4), delicate and pink-flowered with a sweet scent which, when growing in groups,

Figure 3.4 Chalk Fragrant Orchid. Each flower has a characteristic long spur.

can fill the air on a still summer's day. It starts its leafy growth in the spring and flowers in June or July. As with other species, flowering is later further north and at higher altitudes, so in the Peak District, for example, peak flowering is around mid-July. The flower spike, which is quite dense when in full bloom, has a delicate, intricate look, with the long spurs threaded neatly between the flowers.

The Chalk Fragrant grows throughout Britain and Ireland, wherever conditions are suitable, and can occur in large numbers. It avoids shade but, like the Pyramidal Orchid, is quite happy in a longer sward. The important thing is that the sward is cut or grazed once a year, so that it does not build up and smother the spring growth.

The Spotted Orchids

The two Spotted Orchids are named for their spotted leaves - though not all specimens are spotted and sometimes other species have plants with leaf spots! Among the commonest and most beautiful of our native orchids, they are very similar in appearance and are best distinguished by their habitat: the Heath Spotted is found in open, non-shady habitats with wet, more acid soils, while the Common Spotted can be found almost everywhere else. Both species flower over the same period and each can be later or earlier than the other, depending on the situation, aspect, exposure, soil wetness, etc.

Common Spotted Orchid
(*Dactylorhiza fuchsii*)

The flower spike of this orchid is quite variable in size, depending on the age of the plant and the growing conditions in the previous season, but on average it has around 40 flowers. It is generally cylindrical (Fig. 3.5), especially as more flowers appear, but can be very cone-shaped when the flowers first begin to open. The base colour of the flowers varies from white to dark pink (Fig. 3.6), and the lip is generally marked with lines and dashes of dark pink or purple, forming patterns of concentric loops. Entirely white-flowered forms are not uncommon. The lip is three-lobed and the lobes are more or less equal in size.

Figure 3.5 An almost fully open Common Spotted Orchid flower spike.

Figure 3.6 Common Spotted lip and flower colour variation.

Figure 3.7 The attractive leaf spots of the Common Spotted Orchid.

The leaves, which start growing in early spring, are usually spotted all over with chocolate-coloured spots and blotches, making for an attractive plant even without the flowers (Fig. 3.7). It has quite a broad flowering period, from mid-May to the beginning of August, but most plants flower during June or July. Seeds have generally set by mid-August.

Fortunately for gardeners, this beautiful orchid is tolerant in its requirements and is found in a wide range of habitats and soil types. Its range extends from dry slopes to marshes, though not too wet; from chalk and limestone to neutral and mildly acid soils; from south to north, though Cornwall and the far north of Scotland are blank spots; and from grassland to woodland, though usually in the less shady areas. What's more, pollination is very effective and seed production is generally very high, so, once established, one or two 'starter' plants will become very many after a few years, as long as the garden habitat is kept suitable for them. This is the species you are most likely to see on road verges or railway cuttings, and is the most frequent orchid 'volunteer' to crop up in garden lawns.

Heath Spotted Orchid (*Dactylorhiza maculata*)

The Heath Spotted is very similar to the Common Spotted, but a number of differences allow them to be distinguished. The Heath Spotted has a broader and more

Figure 3.8 The Heath Spotted Orchid. The flower shape is broader and 'frillier' than in the Common Spotted.

'blowsy' lip (Fig. 3.8), with a smaller, much less pronounced central lobe, and the lip markings are made of dots and dashes rather than dashes and lines. The flowers are paler – pale pink or lilac – and there are generally fewer of them in the flower spike (no more than 20). The leaf markings tend to be fewer, smaller and rounder, with spots rather than spots and blotches.

The Heath Spotted is usually a smaller plant but equally pretty, with the advantage that it will grow in acid soils; in fact it is the most acid-tolerant of all our recommended native orchids. In nature it is found in a variety of habitats, such as moorland, heathland, raised bogs, grassland and rough pasture, all characterized by their acid soils. In Britain and Ireland it is found mostly in the north and west, which probably reflects the distribution of suitable soil types.

The Marsh Orchids

The Marsh Orchids interbreed readily and are very closely related to the Spotted Orchids, which is why they are placed in the same genus, *Dactylorhiza*. So what distinguishes them? Well, first, the Marsh Orchids tend to occur in wetter situations and second, their leaf-like bracts tend to project beyond the flowers.

Southern Marsh Orchid (*Dactylorhiza praetermissa*)

The flower spike of the Southern Marsh is more crowded than that of the Common Spotted and appears to be much chunkier (Fig. 3.9), becoming cylindrical once in full flower (Fig. 3.10). The flowers are purplish-pink, darker than the Common Spotted but paler than the Northern Marsh, and are marked with dark dots and dashes. The bracts are greenish-purple, and the lower ones project beyond the open flowers.

The Southern Marsh starts growing in early spring and produces about six rather wide, unspotted leaves. Its flowering period is from late May to early July. In our garden meadows these orchids help widen the orchid flowering season, as they start flowering about a week before the Common Spotteds.

This is the commonest Marsh Orchid in the southern half of Britain, and although it is no longer as common as it once was, it

Figure 3.9 The Southern Marsh has a denser flower spike than that of Common Spotted.

Figure 3.10 The spike becomes cylindrical, bearing purplish-pink flowers.

can still occur in large numbers where conditions are right - including industrial sites where limy material has been tipped. Its natural habitat is lowland wet or damp meadows, water meadows, lowland peat bogs, fens and marshes, and also dune slacks where the soil is calcareous, neutral or slightly acid. So it is a good companion species for the Common Spotted Orchid in a garden meadow.

Northern Marsh Orchid (*Dactylorhiza purpurella*)

The Northern Marsh complements the Southern Marsh in its distribution, being predominantly an orchid of the north and west. Only in a few places along the boundary will you find the two species growing together, but they are quite distinct.

The Northern Marsh is one of the shortest of the Marsh Orchids. Its 40 or so flowers are packed into a flat-topped flower spike and are usually a rich deep purple, sometimes magenta or rose. The lip is marked with dots and dashes, like the Spotted Orchids and other Marsh Orchids, but they are not so apparent in the Northern Marsh, as the base colour is so dark (Fig. 3.11). These characteristics are reflected in its old common name, the Dwarf Purple Orchid.

Its leaves are broad and usually unspotted, though in the Welsh subspecies the leaf can be extensively spotted with very dark spots.

Figure 3.11 The Northern Marsh Orchid.

Early Marsh Orchid (*Dactylorhiza incarnata*)

The flowers of the Early Marsh are very distinctive. The lateral petals are held vertically, unlike the other Marsh Orchids and the Spotted Orchids, and the lip is folded vertically. The base colour is often pale and the lip markings are very neat – often complete, concentric lines. So the overall appearance of the flower is slim and elegant. This species also has the largest colour range of any of our native orchids, ranging from pale yellow to bright magenta (Fig. 3.12).

Given its distribution, it's not surprising that the Northern Marsh is somewhat tolerant of acid soils – and it will grow across the range, from calcareous through neutral to slightly acid soils. It is a plant of wet or damp short-turf grassland or any habitat that has similar conditions, such as marshes, water meadows, dune slacks, roadside verges or Machair. Machair is a special habitat found by the coast in the Outer Hebrides. Windblown sand gives the local soil a top dressing of calcareous ground seashell, and the short turf provides a stunning display of wild flowers in early summer.

Gardeners with an acid soil who want an orchid meadow could try a combination of Northern Marsh and Heath Spotted Orchids. Both flower over a similar period. For the Northern Marsh, this is from June to mid-July.

Figure 3.12 A yellowish-pink specimen of an Early Marsh Orchid.

Like our other Marsh Orchids, the leaves are unspotted and rather broad, though in the Early Marsh they tend to be folded, so they appear narrower. Growth starts in the early spring and most flowering occurs between late May and the end of June, with the start of flowering depending on location.

Like the Common Spotted, the Early Marsh is widely distributed throughout Britain and Ireland. However, it is more exacting of the conditions in which it will grow, and so is found far less frequently. It prefers a wet soil with slightly calcareous groundwater and some peat, as well as an open situation. Any habitat where these conditions prevail can provide a home for it - wet meadows, dune slacks, fens, mountain flushes, and so on.

Figure 3.13 *Dactylorhiza* hybrids can be very vigorous.

Marsh and Spotted Orchid hybrids

Members of the genus *Dactylorhiza* are so closely related that they hybridize freely; where any two of the species are grown together, you are likely find hybrids appearing after a few years. The hybrids may not be very fertile, especially if the parents have different chromosome numbers, but they will almost certainly be very vigorous and attractive plants (Figs 3.13 and 3.14). The hybrid shown in Figure 3.14 is a cross between the Common Spotted and the Southern Marsh. The plant was almost 90cm high, with a flower spike approaching 18cm long, which had collapsed under its own weight.

Figure 3.14 A cross between the Common Spotted and Southern Marsh.

Marsh Helleborine (*Epipactis palustris*)

The Helleborines look very different from the species we have discussed so far, and they offer the opportunity to grow orchids in different garden situations. The lip of the Helleborine is in two parts. The cup-shaped rear part (the hypochile) holds the nectar, while the hinged front part (the epichile) attracts the insects and, depending on the species, can be quite elaborate.

In the Marsh Helleborine, some 15 to 20 large flowers are loosely spaced along the flower spike, and they face in more or less the same direction (Fig. 3.15). The lip is white, with pronounced purple veins on the hypochile and a large, frilled epichile with yellow bosses (protuberances). The petals and sepals are a mottled green and purple with white edging. This colour combination gives the appearance of reddish-brown from a distance. The individual flower is absolutely delightful, and mass plantings are very striking indeed.

Mass plantings are quite easy to achieve with this species, because its rhizome branches readily. In older plants, the rhizome system can become quite extensive and produce several flowering shoots each year. Where many plants are growing together, they can blanket the area. This is often true at sites where the Marsh

Figure 3.15 The enchanting flower of the Marsh Helleborine.

Helleborine occurs naturally, if the site remains open without too much competition from other species. Unfortunately for the Marsh Helleborine, it grows in situations where more competitive, taller plants will move in if given the chance, and when this happens the colony will die out. Of course, as gardeners we can prevent this situation.

As its name suggests, the Marsh Helleborine grows in wet or marshy conditions. Its preference is for alkaline groundwater; it will not tolerate acid groundwater. It is quite short for a plant growing in marshy conditions, and does not like shade. The flowering period is usually July, but can stretch from the end of June to the end of August.

Other species for sunny situations

Table 3.4 below gives a brief summary of six other species that are suitable for growing in open situations.

TABLE 3.4. OTHER POSSIBLE SPECIES FOR SUNNY SITUATIONS

Species	Description	Soil conditions	Plant community	Growing notes
Autumn Lady's-tresses	A small rhizomatous plant with a delicate spike of white flowers arranged in a spiral. It is winter green and flowers during late summer.	Prefers dry, nutrient-poor, alkaline soils but will grow on less acidic heathland.	Any grassland where the turf is short, e.g. unimproved pastures, dunes, road verges, lawns.	Long period from germination to flowering (10-15 years), so natural spreading by seed may be very slow. The green plant survives mowing, indeed it needs a short turf, but mowing must stop once the flower spike begins to grow.
Bog Orchid	Our only native orchid with a pseudobulb. It is very small, with tiny green flowers that can open any time between late June and mid-September.	Grows in boggy, usually acidic, areas which are not stagnant and do not dry out. It requires some flow of water.	Often growing amongst a carpet of bog moss (sphagnum) with other specialist plants such as the insectivorous sundew; also with taller vegetation.	Being so small and green, it would be best to grow this orchid in a moss carpet. (Botanists looking for it would be on hands and knees if the ground wasn't so wet!)
Dense-flowered Orchid	The only part of the British Isles in which this Mediterranean species occurs is western Ireland. It is a small-to-medium orchid with tightly clustered, creamy-white flowers. Peak flowering occurs in May. It is winter green.	Prefers calcareous soils that tend to be rocky or gravelly, but sometimes occurs on light, peaty soils over more acidic rocks.	Usually in open habitats such as unimproved pastures, hill grasslands, dunes and road verges, although it sometimes occurs in light woodland.	This species could be an interesting addition to give an early start to the flowering season in an orchid rockery.
Heath Fragrant Orchid	A smaller version of the Chalk Fragrant Orchid (see page 56).	Ranging on soils from mildly acidic to mildly alkaline and sandy to clayey; damp not dry.	Unimproved grassland such as hill pasture, moorland or road verges.	This would be an ideal companion orchid species for the heath spotted orchid, with which it is sometimes found growing.

Irish Lady's-Tresses	Limited distribution in Ireland and Britain. Strangely, its main distribution is in North America. The spiral spike of three rows of delicate white flowers usually opens between late July and early August. It is a short-to-medium, rhizomatous plant.	Mostly on mildly acidic, often peaty, nutrient-poor soils that are permanently damp or wet. Sometimes on neutral or even in alkaline flushes.	Damp meadows and pastures, often amongst taller grasses and rushes which have been kept in check by cattle grazing.	This species very rarely sets seed, so natural spread must rely on vegetative budding of the rhizome and may be very slow.
Narrow-Leaved Marsh Orchid	This is like a smaller, slenderer version of the Southern Marsh (see page 59). Peak flowering for its purplish-pink, more-or-less one-sided flower spike is the first half of June.	This species has quite specific requirements, of wet marshy ground where the groundwater is alkaline-rich.	Fens, water meadows, flushes and marshes in fairly open conditions with sedges and rushes.	One that only the real enthusiast is likely to want to grow, because it has quite specific requirements – very wet, alkaline-rich conditions – and is so similar to the much easier Southern Marsh.

SPECIES SUITABLE FOR SHADY SITUATIONS

In general there are fewer orchids that will grow in shade, and indeed most of those described here, except for the Broad-leaved Helleborine, will often be found growing in open habitats too. As with the species recommended for sunny situations, those recommended for shade are listed broadly in order of their preference for soil moisture, from drier to wetter, but again they all have very similar requirements in this respect. We revisit the subject of orchid species for shady situations in Chapter 8.

Greater Butterfly Orchid
(*Platanthera chlorantha*)

The Greater Butterfly easily wins the prize for the most elegant of our native orchids. Its stately white spires can shine in a shady woodland ride (Fig. 3.16) or dot a flower meadow with delicate highlights.

The flowers are very distinctive and cannot be confused with any other orchid.

Figure 3.16 The graceful Greater Butterfly Orchid.

soil is not too wet. It also occurs in unimproved grassland, especially further north, where it also sometimes strays on to mildly acidic pastures and moorland.

Common Twayblade
(*Neottia ovata*)

The Common Twayblade is an unassuming green orchid with two large, oval, rather fleshy basal leaves – hence the name 'twayblade' (Fig. 3.18). Like most of our orchids, its numbers have been reduced by widespread agricultural improvement, but it is still one of the commonest native orchids and is widely distributed throughout Britain and Ireland.

Each of the small green flowers that adorn the spike has a hood made from the sepals and petals, and a dangling lip that bears a resemblance to a man, as it is deeply forked into two long parallel segments that sometimes have a small tooth in between (Figure 3.17). The leaves appear in the spring, and flowering can occur at any time between mid-May and early August.

Once established, this orchid will form a group of plants, as the underground rhizome produces lateral buds that develop into new plants. This vegetative propagation speeds up colonization, being much faster than growth from self-set seed, which can take many years.

White, washed in places with a pale green, they have a long, strap-like lip and an even longer, thin delicate spur. The structure is designed to attract night-flying moths for pollination, which may also be why the scent is most apparent in the evening and at night. The plant has a basal pair of more or less oval, pale green, unspotted leaves, which start growth in spring. Flowering occurs between late May and late July, depending on habitat and location, tending to be earlier in plants growing in woodland and further south.

The Greater Butterfly Orchid grows throughout Britain and Ireland but is more common at lower altitudes. It has a preference for calcareous soils, and is perhaps most frequently found in woodland where the shade is not too intense – for example, along rides or in clearings – and where the

Figure 3.17 The flowers of the Common Twayblade have a distinctively forked shape.

Figure 3.18 The two basal leaves of the Common Twayblade.

The Common Twayblade grows in a very wide range of habitats, on both limy and slightly acid soils and in both open and shady conditions. It is found in woodland, grassland (with both short and taller sward), among bracken and heather, in dune slacks and on roadside verges.

Like most of our orchids, it grows best in a limy soil. It also probably produces the biggest plants in shade. These characteristics make it a great utility plant for gardeners, and it provides an interesting addition to a patch with native orchids.

Early Purple Orchid

The Early Purple is another orchid with spotted leaves, and in this case the spots are quite large and striking (Fig. 3.19). Its common name is very apt, because it is our earliest-flowering orchid, with purple flowers appearing sometime between early April and early June. The intensity of purple varies, and a population will often include paler specimens (Fig. 3.20) or sometimes white-flowered plants.

Like a number of the other orchid species we have described, the number of flowering spikes of Early Purple can fluctuate markedly from year to year. This is not because they are monocarpic, though some do die after flowering, but due to the plants 'resting' below ground that year. In fact this orchid is quite long-lived, and gardeners can get more predictable flowering from their Early Purples by deadheading them to prevent the exhaustion of food reserves in seed production. Another solution might be to plant Early Purples for several years in succession.

The Early Purple is one of our most

Figure 3.19 The Early Purple Orchid has spotted leaves.

Figure 3.20 A pale-flowered Early Purple.

widespread native orchids, with only a few regions of Britain and Ireland where it is absent or very local. Judging by the huge number of local common names – more than 90 – it must once have been a common and familiar plant. In a few places it can still be seen in large numbers: on the limestone grassland of the Peak District, for example.

As its wide distribution suggests, the Early Purple will grow in a range of soils, excepting only those that are very acid or very wet, and in many situations, as long as the soil remains undisturbed and any shade is not too dense. Grassland and coppiced woodland are its classic habitats.

Broad-leaved Helleborine (*Epipactis helleborine*)

The flowers of the Broad-leaved Helleborine are plain in comparison with those of the Marsh Helleborine (page 63). They are smaller and are normally green with a more-or-less purple lip (Fig. 3.21).

The Broad-leaved is the commonest of our native Helleborines, ranging throughout Britain and Ireland, though it is local in some areas, notably being restricted to the lowlands of Scotland. It is a plant of deciduous woodland or shady areas that mimic woodland, such as hedgerows, parks and gardens.

Figure 3.21 The flowers of the Broad-leaved Helleborine are more subtle than those of its cousin.

It seems the fungal associate of Broad-leaved Helleborine provides a considerable amount of its nutrients and food energy even in the adult plant. The leafy plant is normally quite large, and growing to this size will deplete its reserves to a degree, dependent on the depth of shade in which it is growing. The plant commonly remains below ground for a year or two after flowering, while it builds up its reserves, making it suitable for a shady corner of a garden.

When it does make an appearance above ground, it is rather a late flowerer, usually between mid-July and mid-August. It can start growing quite late in spring as well, appearing as a fairly thick-stemmed shoot curled over at its tip. It then quickly unfurls its characteristic broad oval leaves. By mid- to late September, the drooping fertilized seed capsules are fat and a bright shining green.

The Broad-leaved Helleborine produces seeds that are surprisingly difficult to germinate artificially, and its rhizome is slow-growing. So if you do have one of these orchids in your garden, it is worth nurturing it and any seedlings that appear.

Other species for shady situations

Table 3.5 below provides a summary of another five species that are suitable for shady situations.

IN SUMMARY

This chapter describes the majority of native orchid species that you can easily, and some not so easily, grow in your garden. There are some real beauties among them, and many of these plants have been known to occasionally 'volunteer' in gardens, much to the delight of their owners.

Taken together, they grow across a wide range of conditions, as we have described in detail here, so you should be able to find an orchid for your patch, wherever you live. And once you have them growing successfully, you'll be able to observe much more of their fascinating lives than we have been able to portray in these pages.

Dark-red Helleborine (*Epipactis atrorubens*)

TABLE 3.5. OTHER POSSIBLE SPECIES FOR SHADY SITUATIONS

Species	Description	Soil conditions	Plant community	Growing notes
Creeping Lady's-tresses	An evergreen orchid, small and white-flowered. The more-or-less one-sided flower spike opens between July and August. The plant will spread by the creeping rhizome.	Moist acid or neutral soils with a thick layer of moss and pine needles, and sometimes on old sand dunes beneath pines.	Moderate shade in pine woodland, usually Scots pine.	Creeping Lady's-tresses can fill a niche for gardens that would otherwise be orchid-free.
Dark-red Helleborine	One of the prettier Helleborines, with spikes of dark reddish-purple flowers. A medium-to-tall plant, usually flowering in July.	Mostly found on rocky places on thin alkaline soils overlying limestone.	Typical habitats include rocky hillsides, scree slopes, limestone pavements and cliff ledges. In Europe, the Dark-red Helleborine is often found in woodland.	This could be an interesting species to try in a rockery or in rocky shade.
Green-flowered Helleborine	A medium-to-tall, totally green helleborine. The fresh apple-green stands out in shade. The pendulous flowers open between mid-July and mid-August.	Quite varied, from alkaline soils on chalk or limestone to dry, acidic sands and clays.	Again varied, but always in shade – usually light to moderate, such as in smaller woods, wood margins and hedgerows, and with a rather sparse ground cover.	Perhaps one to try in the shade of a beech tree, which is where it is often found growing in nature.
Lesser Twayblade	A small, rhizomatous orchid with distinctive paired leaves and a spike of a dozen or so small purplish flowers. The flowering period spans mid-May to mid-July.	Wet acidic conditions.	Cool, humid shade, for example moorland on moss carpets beneath straggly heather or damp coniferous or deciduous woodland.	Like the bog orchid, this is another plant that botanists struggle to find and would be shown to best advantage growing on a carpet of moss.
Violet Helleborine	A distinctive medium-to-tall helleborine with a purple washed stem, dark green leaves and very pale green flowers. It flowers late, from mid-July to early September.	Prefers alkaline clay soils overlying calcareous bedrock, although it will grow on sands and gravels and slightly acid soils.	Deciduous woodland, especially beech, hornbeam and oak, often in deep shade. It can tolerate deeper shade than the Broad-leaved Helleborine (see page 68).	The Violet Helleborine will do best in deep soil, because it has a deep root system.

PART TWO

CULTIVATING
ORCHIDS

Chapter Four

Growing
ORCHIDS
in your garden:
the basics

So, you have decided you would like to have a go at growing orchids in your garden, but where do you start? First, think about where you would like to see them - perhaps a naturalistic setting such as a garden meadow, under trees, in a boggy area or in a rockery. Or you might prefer to keep them in a more controlled environment by growing them in containers, beds or borders. The smallest lawn can be turned into a meadow (Fig. 4.1) and borders used to great effect (Fig. 4.2). For a naturalistic look, the choice will depend on the conditions in your garden, and the options are covered in detail in Part 3. This chapter deals with the basics of planting and caring for native orchids.

Opposite: Greater Butterfly Orchid (*Platanthera chlorantha*) and Common Twayblade (*Neottia ovata*) with germander speedwell (*Veronica chamaedrys*). Woodland margin in early June.

Figure 4.1 Orchids in a garden micro-meadow.

As discussed in earlier chapters, orchids take a long time to become established and are dependent on their symbiotic fungal associations. Their roots are both few and substantial, so any damage to them will slow the plant down considerably. This makes them especially vulnerable to disturbance and they will not survive if they are dug up from their growing positions. Care should be taken when planting your orchids, whether directly into the garden or into a pot.

Once orchids are at home in a patch of ground, they will spread readily of their own accord (and you can help them along - see 'Helping your orchids to spread', page 82). It is possible to raise your own plants from seed in isolation, in something akin to laboratory conditions, as described in the next chapter. But starting from scratch, the best approach is to source plants from a reputable supplier.

BUYING YOUR PLANTS

A reputable nursery can supply robust orchid plants grown from seed, and a number of these are listed in Resources. The fact that these plants are home-grown makes them expensive, because of the technical aspects of orchid growth, but they're well worth it. It's also a safe

Figure 4.2 Orchids grown as part of a mixed border in a raised bed.

option, as UK law prohibits digging up plants from the wild (see box on page 96, Chapter 5). Plants grown in open ground and then potted up may have damaged roots, which will be a site for infection and will slow growth. This is because soil has more clay in it than potting compost, making it heavier and stickier and difficult to remove from the roots. Plants raised from seed by a quality supplier will have been potted into a light potting compost, usually based on a John Innes No. 2 with added humus or lime, or into a multipurpose potting compost. Either of these growing media will allow for easy root growth and will not stick to the roots.

Although you can buy orchids from general websites such as eBay, such plants are often sold by individuals who are digging them up from their garden, so it is best to avoid them. We recommend buying them at a specialist plant fair, but check first as not every fair will have an orchid grower. Look for well-established plants, with leaves that are not physically damaged or yellowing. If you want a plant that will flower the same year, expect to pay a bit more for it, as these will be older, sometimes by several years. The stallholder will be delighted to help you with this, as orchid growers, like all gardeners, are passionate about their subject and keen to welcome new enthusiasts.

Hardy orchids are sometimes available at garden centres, but these often lack details. The plants may be labelled as *Dactylorhiza*, for example, but not specify which of the many species in this genus it is. Very often they are hybrids, as these are faster-growing and produce larger plants. While such plants are fine for cultivation in the garden, avoid them if you want a naturalized meadow, as they may not be native species and may be sterile if they are hybrids.

PLANTING AND CARING FOR YOUR ORCHIDS

If you buy plants in pots, planting them out couldn't be simpler. For planting into a lawn, border, flowerbed or uncultivated ground, use a bulb planter or a trowel with a round section to take out a plug the same size as your plant pot. Knock the plant out of the pot with all the compost and – taking care not to disturb the roots – put it straight into the prepared hole. This should give the orchid a good start: no root disruption means there should be no brake on growth and development.

Whichever type of orchid you have, avoid planting it so deep that the bottom leaves are at ground level; or that the bud is completely below ground level if the orchid is dormant when you put it in. This is contrary to the way that many of these plants grow in the wild, but until the plant is established, it needs to be cosseted so that it does not succumb to infection.

Should you feed your orchids?

If you are growing your orchids in pots or beds where there is no immediate competition from surrounding vegetation, an application of fertilizer can make a very direct and obvious difference to growth. You can see this in Figure 4.3. The two orchids are both four years old, having been set up in sterile culture from seed on the same day. After three years the plant on the right was watered with a half-strength liquid fertilizer, applied six times in a single year. The plant on the left was watered as normal, without fertilizer. These plants now produce delightful flowers.

In contrast, if you put fertilizer on orchids naturalized in a lawn or meadow, they will be swamped by the more vigorous grass

Figure 4.3. Two Common Spotted Orchids of identical age. The larger plant has been treated with a weak fertilizer six times in a single year.

and other meadow plants. Likewise, if you use commercial potting compost when planting orchids, the fertilizer in the compost will aid the more rapid growth of surrounding plants, crowding out the orchids.

In subsequent years they will grow just as they would in the wild.

If the plant you have bought is bare-rooted, as they often are when sent through the post, the orchid will still have its symbiotic fungus on its roots. In this condition the ground needs to be carefully prepared to ensure minimal damage to the roots and ensure that the plants establish themselves as quickly as possible. Dig a hole and make sure the soil is broken up into as fine a tilth as possible. You can now 'pot up' the plant into your ground using the fine soil as the potting compost. When planting up an area for naturalizing, don't be tempted to use commercial potting composts as these often contain fertilizer, which will stimulate competing vegetation. Once planted, a good watering will do the orchids a world of good as long as you don't feed them (see box opposite).

Skilled growers keep their plants in loose compost so they can be easily taken out and packed in moss for postal delivery. Not only does this keep the cost of delivery down but it also avoids the risk of the compost moving in transit and exposing the orchid's roots or shoots to damage. If packed in moss, the plant is effectively bare-rooted and should be treated as such when it arrives.

Your soil type will partly influence the species of orchids you can grow in your garden

Figure 4.4 Cutting and digging a small square hole suitable for refilling with an appropriate compost. If it is done with care, a clean hole can be made every time.

(see page 52). If you have any doubts about the suitability of your soil, then remove the soil as though a big pot was going to be put in and fill the hole with a compost that is more appropriate for the species you wish to grow (see 'Choosing composts', page 86). This is shown in Figure 4.4, where a hole was cut into clay and filled with a compost suited to chalk-hill species. If, as pictured, the soil is a solid clay, it is important to match the compost to the surroundings, otherwise the contents of the hole will be much lighter than the ground and it is likely to fill with water drained from the surroundings. This is easily solved by taking soil from elsewhere in the garden, breaking it down to a fine tilth, then using it as the base for a compost mix designed for the species being planted.

Assessing your growing conditions

To test the pH of your soil, a proprietary soil-pH-testing kit is a good start. Some species are very easy-going about their soil acidity – for example, the Spotted and Marsh Orchids of the genus *Dactylorhiza*. Others prefer it a little more alkaline, such as the Bee Orchid and Pyramidal Orchid, both associated with chalk areas in the wild. It is only at extremes of soil acidity or alkalinity that you can be certain some species will not thrive. Chapter 3 provides details of the preferred conditions for different species.

For all of the species that don't have 'Marsh' or 'Bog' in their name, the one thing to avoid is permanently wet ground. The Marsh Orchids are generally quite comfortable growing with their feet in water, but they don't have to. It is important to recognize the difference between wet and waterlogged: waterlogged soil tends to have a static water content, which gradually loses its dissolved oxygen to microbial respiration of any organic matter in the soil. The result is a stagnant soil with anaerobic sludge, which is unable to support plant growth. When orchids grow in the wild in situations where the soil is permanently wet, the water tends to be moving through the soil and the organic content will be low. An extreme example is where a spring appears above ground to form a pool. This can be a favourite site for some species, like the Marsh Orchids; and Common Spotted Orchids can be quite happy sitting in water, as long as it is well aerated. But this can become a problem in winter, when the water may freeze, causing damage to the roots.

Figure 4.5 Marsh Helleborines like damp conditions and a sunny spot where they can thrive on their creeping rhizome.

Deadheading

Some species, such as the Bee Orchid, tend to flower once in the wild and then rest below ground for a year or more. They can be encouraged to flower more regularly by deadheading immediately after their flowers have started to shrivel. Similarly, deadheading orchids that *do* flower regularly will also give you bigger flower spikes in the next growing season. Once you have a fair few orchids in your patch, deadhead a proportion each year. Those that you leave will produce more than enough seed for the generation of new plants.

Ideally, whether or not you deadhead the flowers, leave the rest of the green shoot to wither and die back naturally, because it will still be feeding the underground storage organ, allowing the orchid to build up maximum reserves for next season's flower. On the other hand, if your orchid patch has finished flowering and you want to cut the whole area down, then doing so after the seed has set will not stop the plants flowering in the next season (see Chapter 7, page 130). This is what we do with our meadows.

Some of the Helleborines also like a damp environment – for example, our Marsh Helleborine (Fig. 4.5) and its hardy relative from North America, the Stream Orchid. (Although not a native orchid of Britain, the latter grows well in our climate and is a popular species for growing in the garden. While the name implies that the plant is large, it rarely achieves a metre in height; usually it will be half that.) Both of these orchids have roots that grow relatively close to the surface, and they do not do well if the soil dries out.

Watering

For most orchid species grown in a garden, it isn't necessary to water established plants in open ground. The exceptions are species that naturally grow in wet situations, but in the garden are being grown in a well-drained soil. These can be affected by drought, and they need to be watered on a regular basis when the weather is dry. It is easy to think that this occurs only in summer, but spring can be dry in Britain and Ireland and, though cool, this is when your plants are waking up and will need moisture.

General care

Once your orchids are growing well, they can be left to themselves. If the plants are established in a lawn, cutting can involve tricky manoeuvres with a mower; or you could use shears to trim around the plants so they're not accidentally flattened. Avoid using a strimmer, as these are indiscriminate and hard to control. (For details of how and when to cut a flower meadow, see Chapter 7.) Once plants are established, the soil should not be disturbed, even if the orchids don't appear for a year. Very often they will reappear later from a dormant plant.

You may encounter a few problems with pests and diseases, though your orchids will be no more vulnerable than any other garden plants. We return to this subject in Chapter 6.

HELPING YOUR ORCHIDS TO SPREAD

Waiting for your orchids to spread naturally is a slow business, but one which repays patience, as the plants will be present exactly where they are best suited to be (Fig. 4.6). Sometimes, though, it is quicker to give them a helping hand in increasing their numbers - either by broadcasting seed or by dividing clumps.

Direct-sowing orchid seed

As we saw in Chapter 2, conditions have to be just right for orchid seed to germinate. Orchids produce vast amounts of seed, only a few of which will find a suitable place to grow, given the right fungal partner.

If you have even just a few established orchids, chances are the local conditions will be right for some seeds to grow and you may find that volunteer plants will appear in the most charming places - as illustrated by the orchid in Figure 4.8. Once our meadows were in full production and we allowed the orchids to do their own thing, we found that a neighbour, a relaxed gardener who occasionally pulled up a few weeds, had a beautiful display of Southern Marsh Orchids in her large alpine trough.

To encourage your orchids to naturalize, collect the ripe seed heads from your orchids before they dehisce (split open), take them indoors, break them open to release the seed into a paper envelope, then wait for a still day to scatter them close to the ground. See Chapter 5 for details of how to collect and store seed.

Figure 4.6 A thriving colony of Common Spotted Orchids at a meadow's edge.

In the moist environment outdoors, the seed must find a fungal partner quickly before it loses its viability. If the vegetation cover is thick where the seed lands, it is unlikely to be able to do this. In our orchid meadows, a favourite place for new orchids to appear is on the edges of a trampled path. In a local wood, a bridle path that was heavily used by horse riders had most of its Spotted Orchids growing where the trampling had been intense over the autumn and winter (this is pictured in Figure 8.4 on page 138).

So if you want to help your orchids reproduce in a naturalistic setting such as a meadow, the best time to distribute the seeds is after the patch has been cut down for the autumn and there has been some rain, so the ground is soft. It might even be helpful to do a bit of stomping around in your wellys once the seeds have been sown.

Dividing clumps

If your orchids have grown into clumps, these can be divided to increase the number of plants and spread them over a wider area. For rhizomatous species, it is best to do this in spring, when the new green shoots are just beginning to appear. Plants with pseudobulbs can be divided at the beginning of the resting period. Extreme care must be taken to keep root disturbance to a minimum. Take a large chunk of earth containing the whole clump, split it as gently as possible, then replant immediately. The Marsh Helleborine can be split in this way, as can its American cousin, the Stream Orchid (Fig. 4.7). Being non-native, the latter should not be used in a naturalized setting like a garden meadow, but it does do well in pots and containers, self-seeding and forming extensive clumps in the right setting.

Figure 4.7 An established plant of the Stream Orchid, a hardy native of North America. This species, like most Helleborines, grows from a creeping rhizome and is easier to transplant than many of the deep-rooting species. Species growing from rhizomes are all easy to transplant and divide.

Species with tubers do not often form clumps, and where they do the tubers will be close together and the roots intertwined. In these cases, just enjoy the massed beauty of the clump rather than trying to split it, which is likely to cause significant damage. If you are determined to try, dig out a large chunk of earth, gently wash the soil off in a bowl of water, untangle the roots and then pull the plants apart.

GROWING ORCHIDS IN CONTAINERS

If you are short of space, or you just want to bring your orchids nearer to the window, then grow your plants in containers. Starting off with container growing is also a good way of getting to know the foibles, tastes and growing cycles of your orchids, which is invaluable as a basis for larger-scale cultivation.

Your garden soil may not be suitable for direct planting of some species, notably the lime-loving ones associated with chalk hillsides,

Green-winged Orchids
(*Anacamptis morio*).

Figure 4.8 The tiniest garden can have an orchid. Here, a Southern Marsh Orchid has self-set with a bonsai tree.

Figure 4.9 Frost damage to terracotta pots left outside over winter

so container growing is a good option. Two favourite species for such treatment are the Bee Orchid and the Pyramidal Orchid.

Some orchid species will self-set not only into their own pots but also into adjacent ones, if the compost is left undisturbed for long periods. Marsh Orchids will often seed into pots containing ferns or hostas, as these have similar requirements for soil type and dampness (see 'Companion plants', page 88); and these plants tend to be left for several years while they settle in and develop their full grace and beauty - perfect conditions for volunteer orchid plants. Such occurrences are a delightful surprise, often going unnoticed until the orchid flowers (Fig. 4.8).

Choosing containers

Besides container size and shape, the material is an important consideration. Weight is one of the major factors, as large pots will be almost immovable once they are filled with damp compost.

The main options for commercially available pots are:

- terracotta and glazed pottery
- metal
- plastic and fibreglass
- wood
- concrete, stone and reconstituted stone.

Terracotta pots and moulded rectangular troughs have a quality that is difficult to beat: they age well, and look good when they have lichen or moss growing on them. Frost damage can be a problem (Fig. 4.9), though more expensive frost-resistant forms are available. Unglazed terracotta is also quick to dry out in summer, but again, vitrified forms impervious to water are available.

Glazed pots are nearly always frost-resistant and simple to clean. They also look good in multiple displays, their glazed colours contrasting with other pots or with the colour of the flowers.

Metal pots and containers are usually large and heavy, so once in position they are rarely moved. You wouldn't generally plant directly into them, but use them as a snug container for

Figure 4.10 A fibreglass container structured to look like cast iron, from a nineteenth-century design.

Figure 4.12 A modern version of the Versailles box.

Figure 4.11 A traditional Versailles box containing a citrus tree. This will be moved inside as winter approaches, to the benefit of both the wooden container and the tree.

a plastic pot. The oldest form of this type of container is a cast-iron urn.

Plastics and fibreglass containers are durable and light (Fig. 4.10), so the weight of the finished display will be almost entirely comprised of the weight of the compost.

Wood is an attractive material and makes for a soft and decorative background for your orchid planting. This type of planter reaches its pinnacle with the Versailles box (Figs 4.11 and 4.12). A disadvantage of wood is rot, but a plastic liner helps.

Concrete, stone and reconstituted stone containers are heavy. The weight of the compost may turn out to be a small proportion of the total weight, so moving them is likely to be quite an undertaking.

Choosing composts

A number of orchid species are happy growing in all sorts of soils, and companion plants in a container need not be restricted by the choice of growing medium, so shop-bought composts are suitable, but you may prefer to make up your own (see box opposite). See Table 3.3 on page 52, Chapter 3, for a summary of the soil requirements of our recommended native orchid species.

Commercially available composts generally fall into two categories: soil- or loam-based, and soil-less or multipurpose. John Innes No. 2 is of most interest to the grower of hardy orchids in the garden. It is a loam-based general-purpose compost, which works well for most houseplants and vegetables grown in pots. It has the right level of fertilizer added to suit established plants that don't want disturbance. This is the basis for many of the composts used for native orchids (but not tropical epiphytes). As it is loam-based, it can be easily adapted to the desired alkalinity (pH above 7) and if it dries out, it is easier to re-wet than peat-based or multipurpose composts.

For some native orchids, namely most of the *Dactylorhiza* species (the Northern, Southern and Early Marsh, and the Common Spotted and Heath Spotted), soil-less multipurpose composts with a high humus content are ideal, because these most closely mimic the soils they commonly grow in, so will result in strong plants. As a home-made alternative to commercial soil-less composts (often based on peat, the extraction of which has a serious ecological impact), make leaf mould - see box below. While a highly organic compost is ideal for some species, these composts tend to be acidic, so you can add garden lime for species that require it (see below).

Mixing your own potting compost

By mixing your own compost, you can tailor it to the combination of plants you are planning to grow. Here we describe the mixes we have found to be successful, and we suggest various components you could try adding. Don't be too concerned about the exact amounts of the materials, as well-established orchids are remarkably tolerant. On the other hand, as orchids don't like being disturbed, any experimentation should not be too extreme. If the orchid is not growing well, top-dress the compost to adjust the balance of nutrients; but if your mix is clearly a failure, it is better to repot the orchid, despite the risk.

Generally the starting point is a loam, usually John Innes No. 2, but the turned soil from molehills makes a good alternative base.

For species suited to alkaline soils, add garden lime. The exact amount of lime to loam will vary, but mixing John Innes No. 2 with the same amount of garden lime will create a good calcareous mixture ideally suited to chalk-hill species. For a less alkaline mix, 2 parts loam to 1 part garden lime is not unusual, or 3 parts loam to 1 part lime.

For species which like a neutral or only slightly alkaline soil - for example, the Early Purple Orchid and Green-winged Orchid - a mix of 2 parts John Innes No. 2 and 1 part multipurpose compost is good. Add to this 1 part

Making leaf mould

Simply fill bin liners or a compost bin with leaves. As long as they are damp, but not waterlogged, after a year you will have a superb humus. This can be chopped or sieved to break up the remaining leafy bits, then used as a soil-less compost base. Avoid the thick leaves of horse chestnut and sycamore, as they break down too slowly.

garden lime for every 4 parts of mix to solve the problem of compost that is too acidic.

The following are other additives for orchid compost mixtures, which we have used with some success. They are all suited to pots and containers that will be kept outside all year round.

- **Composted bark.** This is good for water retention, but if it dries out completely it can be difficult to re-wet.
- **Sphagnum moss.** This works well as an additive in soil-less composts where improved water retention is required, but it breaks down very quickly.
- **Grit, sand (not builders'), pumice and perlite.** Add these materials to the mix for orchids that like a well-drained compost. Being mineral, they will not materially change over the lifetime of the planted pot.
- **Charcoal.** This 'sweetens' compost by binding any breakdown products, lightens the compost and aids water retention.
- **Material from the compost heap.** This is excellent stuff and, if you have a nice big container to fill, it can be a useful part of the recipe. But be careful, as it rots away quickly. It can also introduce unwelcome guests into the container, like slugs, snails and fungal diseases.

In containers and pots, where you can control the growth of other plants so they don't overcrowd your orchids, a judicious use of fertilizer can give lovely displays of foliage and flowers.

Companion plants in containers and pots

There are some excellent planting combinations for orchids in pots, suggestions for which are summarized in Table 4.1 on page 91.

Some of these may seem unlikely, such as hostas (Fig. 4.13) and Marsh Orchids, but in fact the orchids thrive under the permanent protection of the hostas. Plant a Marsh Orchid, or any other *Dactylorhiza* species, towards the front of the pot, with one of the smaller hosta species behind it to bring out the colour of the flower. A number of relatively small hostas are suitable: examples are 'Blue Moon', which reaches a height of about 12cm; curled plantain lily, which grows to 75cm; and 'Ginko Craig', at 30cm.

Another suitable plant to grow in containers with Marsh Orchids, as long as there is some shade available, is the Himalayan or evergreen maidenhair fern. This combination can also

Figure 4.13 Hostas make very good companion plants for species such as Marsh Orchids, as their compost and water requirements are much the same.

be used for the Common Spotted and Heath Spotted Orchids.

Since you will be trying to minimize disturbance of your container orchids, you could mix them with other perennials that can extend the season. The smaller species of *Dicentra*, such as squirrel corn or Dutchman's breeches, are good for early-season blooms, while varieties of bugle with colourful foliage, for example 'Variegata' or 'Atropurpurea', provide interest to the end of the year.

The two earliest orchids to flower are the Early Purple and the Green-winged (Figs 4.14 and 4.15). Neither are tall plants - 40cm being a

> *Since you will be trying to minimize disturbance of your container orchids, you could mix them with other perennials that can extend the season.*

Figure 4.14 Early Purple Orchids.

Figure 4.15 Green-winged Orchids.

good height for the flower spike - so it is worth keeping the associated plants short. These species do well with grasses such as perennial quaking grass or the shorter annual hare's tail grass, which seeds very freely. Arrange them in the container to give both height and contrast to the colour of the orchid flower.

Being active growers in the spring, both the Early Purple and Green-winged Orchids are also worth pairing up with primroses, cowslips and, best of all, bluebells. Around the rim of your pots, you can soften the edge with the addition of creeping Jenny (Fig. 4.16), though keep it in check or it can easily become dominant.

The Greater Butterfly Orchid is one of the most delightful and elegant of our native species, complemented beautifully by the simple charm of our cornflower. It also grows well with pincushion lucida, a perennial lilac-flowered scabious that grows to 20cm; and Stoke's aster, another pretty flower with a cornflower-like

Figure 4.16 Creeping Jenny. This can become invasive if not kept under control.

Figure 4.17 Love-in-a-mist, also known as nigella.

Figure 4.18 Devil's bit scabious with a comma butterfly.

Figure 4.19 Greater knapweed. The flower is larger and more open than that of common knapweed.

appearance. Blue cupidone is a plant with fine foliage and a cornflower-like flower that also complements the Butterfly Orchid. In a sunny spot, the foliage of coriander adds distinctive colour and interest to a display.

Plants that fit in well with Pyramidal Orchids and Bee Orchids include cornflowers, scabious and love-in-a-mist (Fig 4.17). Blue flax (*Linum perenne*) is an upright slender perennial with blue flowers that grows to about 30cm and will flower throughout the summer, making it a rewarding companion in a display.

If you have a substantial pot or container devoted to growing native orchids, consider turning it into a tiny area of native wild flowers that you would expect to find growing with your orchids in the wild. These might include meadow buttercup, ragged robin and hawkbits.

The paintings shown at the start of each chapter of the book can also be used for

Figure 4.20 The Broad-leaved Helleborine is one orchid that would suit a container in a shady corner.

inspiration, because they show our recommended orchids with other wild flowers that commonly grow with them. Keep your wild flower area flowering into autumn by adding later-flowering perennials such as devil's bit scabious (Fig. 4.18) or greater knapweed (Fig. 4.19).

For containers in shady corners, try mixing Broad-leaved Helleborines (Fig. 4.20) and Early Purple Orchids with a herb like basil.

IN SUMMARY

Growing orchids in your garden isn't difficult, and if you follow our guidance in this chapter, you have every chance of success. Source good healthy plants, so that they can be expected to flower within a year or two, and if you want to sow your own orchid seed, be patient, as the natural growth process is slow. Prepare your soil or compost with the needs of the particular species in mind, and minimize disturbance once your orchids are planted out. So if you are growing in containers, take time to choose the right one for your garden and planting combination.

Orchids can be complemented beautifully with other cultivated species or wild flowers, in containers or in borders. We have included a number of ideas for container-scale combinations to get you started, but the scope for creativity is endless.

TABLE 4.1. SUGGESTED COMPANION PLANTS FOR ORCHIDS IN CONTAINERS

Orchid species	Companion plants
Common Spotted Orchid	Creeping Jenny, *Dicentra* (smaller species), evergreen maidenhair, hostas, lobelia
Early Purple Orchid	Bluebell, creeping Jenny, hare's tail grass, primrose, quaking grass
Greater Butterfly Orchid	Blue cupidone, coriander, cornflower, pincushion lucida, Stokes' aster
Green-winged Orchid	Cowslip, creeping Jenny, hare's tail grass, quaking grass
Pyramidal and Bee Orchids	Blue flax, cornflower, love-in-a-mist, scabious
Southern Marsh Orchid	Bugle, *Dicentra* (smaller species), hostas, marsh marigold

Chapter Five

Raising PLANTS from seed

If you would like to grow orchids from seed yourself, you can do it in two ways.

- Scatter seed direct on the ground, as described in the last chapter. This does, however, require access to a large amount of seed, and takes a lot of patience, as the natural life cycle of orchids is long.

- Grow the seed in sterile culture. This is rather more involved, but is more reliable and also quicker, as you can grow the plants throughout the year instead of being restricted to the natural growing season. The seeds get all the nutrients they need to germinate and grow into small plants, which you can then pot up for planting out. It's a very good way of generating more plants for your garden or for larger-scale repopulation projects (see Chapter 10).

This chapter deals exclusively with growing in culture, though the section 'Collecting seed' (page 95), is also relevant to direct seed scattering.

Opposite: Common Spotted Orchid (*Dactylorhiza fuchsii*) with tufted vetch (*Vicia cracca*), yellow rattle (*Rhinanthus minor*) and crested dog's-tail (*Cynosurus cristatus*). Meadow in mid-June.

GROWING FROM SEED IN CULTURE

Growing orchids from seed in culture chiefly involves getting the seed to germinate and then transferring the seedlings into pots and getting them to grow on. Both stages can be challenging, but the difficulty varies markedly between species, so it is worth starting off with an easy one!

Figure 5.1 shows the relative ease of cultivation for our recommended species (as described in Chapter 3). For example, the Common Spotted Orchid is at the bottom left of the chart, as this is an easy species both to germinate and to grow on, whereas the Greater Butterfly Orchid,

at the top right, is quite tricky at both stages. The Helleborines are difficult to get started (because they seem to have a natural germination inhibitor present) but once germinated are not too difficult to grow on.

The seeds are germinated in a sterile growth medium, but first the outside of the seed must be sterilized to rid the whole system of stray fungal and bacterial spores. Note that growing in culture involves no symbiotic fungus. Instead, a complete nutrient medium is used, which supplies the seeds with all their needs. This is the easiest way to get the seeds started, and our own experience tells us that once they

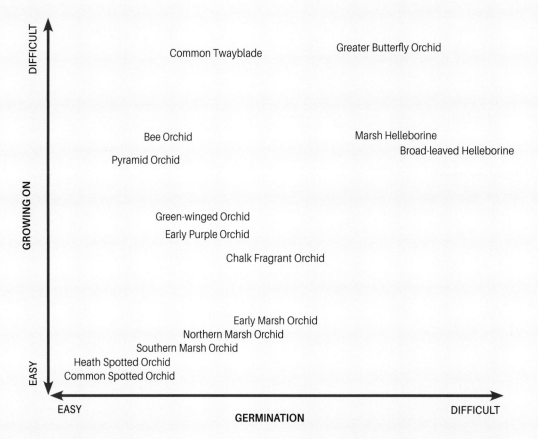

Figure 5.1 The relative ease of germinating orchid seeds and growing the plants on. Some species are fairly easy to germinate and grow on, others are harder to grow on than to germinate, and yet others are difficult from the start.

are independent plants, the orchids will pick up their fungal associate from the soil if they need it. When orchids germinate in the wild, they are *usually* no longer dependent on their fungal associate to provide nutrients once the seedlings have started to produce chlorophyll. But some species, like the Butterfly Orchid, need a fungal associate throughout their lives.

Growing from seed in culture is not like ordinary gardening, and requires some unusual equipment, listed below. Make sure you have everything you need before you start, and as backup it's worth having duplicates of items in this list, especially anything breakable or spillable.

Equipment you will need:
- Light rubber gloves
- Methylated spirits
- Forceps (two pairs)
- Thin metal spatula
- Small sharp knife (for green pods)
- Thin chlorine bleach (i.e. ordinary domestic bleach)
- Tissue paper (optional) for wrapping seeds during sterilization
- Aluminium foil
- Glass jars (several)
- Sterile surface and a cabinet or enclosed area to restrict air currents.

GROWING FROM SEED IN CULTURE: A STEP-BY-STEP GUIDE

There are several stages involved in growing from seed in culture:
1. Collecting seed
2. Storing and preserving seed
3. Setting up and sterilizing the work area
4. Choosing and sterilizing the growth medium
5. Sterilizing seed
6. Germinating seed
7. Transplanting seedlings and growing them on to a flowering plant

Growing orchid seed in culture has the advantage of a very high germination rate and the disadvantage that it requires a knowledge of sterile techniques, because you are providing all the nutrients for growth under sterile conditions. Since even a single fungal or bacterial spore will grow in the nutrient mixture for the orchid seeds, all spores must be excluded.

It's a little tricky to cultivate your own orchids in this way and it requires some specific equipment and skill, but it turns orchid growing into an exciting and absorbing occupation, with an immense sense of achievement when you succeed with your first flowering orchid.

Stage 1. Collecting seed

Before collecting orchid seed, there are some very important points to consider.
- If the plants are growing on private property, you must seek permission from the landowner.
- You may damage the plant unless you are very careful. Do not pull the seed pods off: either pinch them or cut them off cleanly.
- Some species are specifically protected by law and seed collection from these is not allowed. These species are listed in the box on page 96.

The first time you start to grow orchids, we advise you only use seed from abundant plants, as you may not be immediately successful and you don't want to waste precious seeds from scarce plants. Practise only with abundant seed taken from an acceptable site, such as from an orchid already established in a garden. Once you have been growing orchids from seed for a while and can be sure of a successful outcome, you can help the conservation of species by returning the plants grown from seeds you collected to the original site, or to another site so that their range increases.

Because of the challenges of growing from seed, it isn't really worth buying seed online, as the cost per seed is prohibitive and there is no guarantee that it is viable. But if you do want to purchase seed, before you try growing it, have a good look at it to check that it is viable (see box opposite).

There are two methods of seed collecting:
a) Collect seed when the orchid has completed its flowering cycle and the seed pods are ripe – they will either be already split or about to split.
b) Collect the seed pods when they are still green.

Once you have collected the seeds, don't forget to label them immediately, with species, date and place where they were collected.

Method A. Collecting seed from ripe seed pods

This method works well, because the seed is definitely mature and ready to grow. Most of our native orchid species produce mature seed about 6-10 weeks after pollination, depending on the weather. When the weather is dry and the seed pod mature, the pod will split and release the seed to be dispersed on the wind. If you collect the seed at this point, you'll need to store it safely. See Figure 5.2 for a neat way to create an envelope that has no open corners through which the seeds can escape.

Seed pods ripen from the bottom of the flower stem upwards, reflecting the likely opening sequence of the flowers and therefore

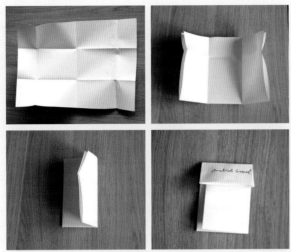

Figure 5.2 How to fold a sheet to save and store orchid seed without losing any of the tiny seeds in corners.

Figure 5.3 Some species, such as Pyramidal Orchids, often have a higher proportion of non-viable seeds.

Checking that seed is viable

This method applies only to seeds collected from ripe pods, not green pods. Once you have collected your ripe seed, examine each seed using a hand lens or a low-power microscope, to check that it is potentially viable. There should be a visible embryo inside the seed net (Fig. 5.4). Some pods will produce what looks like seed but in fact they contain no embryo, just the surrounding seed coat, or testa. A practised eye can identify the dud seed pods, but a quick look with a lens will easily confirm the diagnosis.

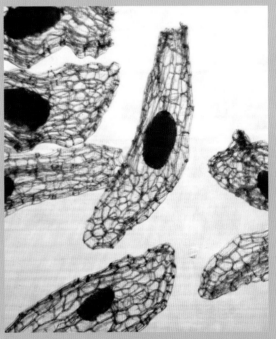

Figure 5.4 Most of these seeds from a Southern Marsh Orchid are viable, with an obvious dark embryo in the middle of the supporting net. The seed that is partially visible at the bottom right of the picture lacks the embryo and is not viable.

pollination sequence. If the bottom pods have already split, it should be possible to find some in perfect condition just above the last one that has opened.

Not all seeds get pollinated, so after collection of the seeds, check for the presence of an embryo (see box on the right). In general, unpollinated or maldeveloped seed pods don't attain the full-sized roundness of pods containing viable seed, so with practice it's possible to tell from the pods themselves. Look at plants in the field to learn how to recognize the viable seed pods, as these can be mingled in with seedless pods on the same flowerhead. This seems to happen more often with some species than others - the Pyramidal Orchid (Fig. 5.3) is one such low-seed producer.

Method B. Collecting seed from green seed pods

Collecting and sowing 'in the green' works better for some species, and has advantages when it comes to sowing seed in culture. The main advantage is that because the pods haven't split, their contents will be sterile, so when growing the seed in culture it isn't necessary to sterilize the seeds but simply to sterilize the outside of the capsule before opening it and removing the seeds (see page 103 ['Sterilizing seed']).

Species worth collecting in the green are in the genus *Ophrys*; the Bee Orchids and their relatives. In Britain this is really only *O. apifera* (our Bee Orchid - see Figs 5.5 and 5.6, as there

Figure 5.6 Bee Orchids have very distinctive seed pods – among the largest seed pods of the British orchids.

Figure 5.5 Bee Orchids can be successfully grown from seeds taken from green seed pods. In the British Isles, most Bee Orchids are self-pollinated.

are too few of the others to disturb, but in Continental Europe other *Ophrys* species are more common and can be collected if local rules allow. Collect pods about 3cm above the topmost split pod on the plant.

However, it's worth remembering that while seed collected when seed pods are about to split will definitely be ripe, you cannot be certain that seed collected in the green will germinate - even if it would have been viable if left to fully ripen on the plant. So collecting and sowing in the green introduces another variable into an already complex formula.

Stage 2. Storing and preserving seed

Because seeds collected in the green have not matured, they cannot enter a state of dormancy so will remain viable for only a very short period. Therefore sow them soon after collection.

On the other hand, mature, ripe seeds can be stored dry for more than a year under the right conditions. An easy way to dry them and keep them dry is to put the paper envelope containing the seeds into a sealed jar with a desiccant, in its own paper packet. Do not mix different seeds, because you will never be able to separate them afterwards. For long-term storage, put the whole jar in a fridge or freezer.

Any simple desiccant will suffice, but avoid using silica gel as it can over-dry the seed and render it useless. Some desiccant options are:
Salt, dried in the oven to remove all moisture
Rice, also thoroughly heat-dried
Anhydrous calcium chloride (available as a water treatment for swimming pools)

Once dry, ripe seeds will remain viable for several months at room temperature, longer in a refrigerator and for years in a freezer. Loss of seed viability is normally associated with incorrect storage and consequent mould growth, specifically if the seed is damp. So only store dry seed, and if it has to be at room temperature, keep it in the dark and not in a plastic bag.

Stage 3. Setting up and sterilizing the work area

Before you start, it is essential to sterilize everything – work areas, tools and material. If not, the seed culture will be contaminated with fungus or bacteria, and, because the growth medium is so nutritious, the contamination will spread rapidly throughout the culture. The different types of infection problem that you may come across in your growth culture can be broadly categorized as follows:

Appearance of infection	Probable origin
Grey-yellow slime, usually bacteria	From your hands
Cultures infected with the same type of fungus on the surface	Either: a) contaminated seed or b) a local source of infection shedding spores
Occasional infection of different types	Airborne infection
Infections in the growth medium, rather than on the surface	Contaminated growth medium

From the list above, you can see that fungal and bacterial infections of the media can start anywhere, from solid surfaces to spores shaken off clothes, so you need to take great care. Fungal spores and bacteria are so small that tracking down their source precisely is virtually impossible, but by observing the following guidelines on technique, it should be possible to produce clean and productive seed cultures.

The work area

When designing your work zone, observing two key points will make a happy result more likely. The first is that all the surfaces of the work area should be smooth and easily wiped clean, so don't use wooden, porous or tiled surfaces, though you can use a sheet of glass to cover them. The surfaces must be sterile.

The second point is that the work area needs to be as draught-free as possible, so that

Green-winged Orchid (*Anacamptis morio*).

movement of dust and dirt in the air is kept to a minimum. Although it is possible to carry out the process on an open table, it is difficult, because there are too many airborne bacteria and fungal spores around. It is much better to use a fish tank as an improvised cabinet, or a sheet of glass supported above the work surface with a plastic curtain taped down on three sides.

A rectangular fish tank laid on its side provides hard, smooth inside surfaces that can be completely sterilized before use. Half-close the front opening with a piece of plastic that can be folded out of the way so you can move materials in and out of the box. With this system, your movements should be very calculated and slow, otherwise air currents will draw contaminating microorganisms into your work cabinet.

For the more serious, the best system is undoubtedly the laminar flow cabinet. Although expensive, it provides a sterile work environment. These sterile cabinets come in different classifications for different uses. For plant work of this sort, all you need is a clean and sterile atmosphere, so buy the cheapest flow cabinet with the lowest classification (Fig. 5.7).

You can build your own flow cabinet suitable for plant work. The only difficulty would be providing and correctly installing a filter capable of removing bacteria and fungal spores from the incoming air.

Work surfaces should be sterilized using a solution of 70 per cent methylated spirits to 30 per cent water. Use a tissue soaked in this mix to wipe the surfaces down. When working with methylated spirits, wear rubber gloves as protection for your skin, which will be dried out by exposure to the alcohol.

Sterilizing tools

Each time you set up seeds you will need:
- two pairs of metal forceps
- a thin metal spatula
- a small knife (if using green pods)

This equipment, once wrapped in aluminium foil (see Figures 5.8 and 5.9), can be sterilized using dry heat. This can be done in the kitchen oven: heat up the tools to 180°C for 45 minutes. Alternatively, you could use a pressure cooker. Sterilize them at 121°C for 30 minutes. This is more or less 1 atmosphere overpressure, and is the maximum domestic-pressure-cooking pressure. It will ensure complete sterility.

Figure 5.7 A purpose-built laminar flow cabinet – perfect for botanical work.

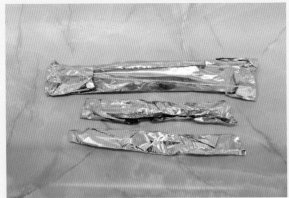

Figure 5.8 Wrap up instruments for sterilization, making sure no parts are open to the air.

Figure 5.9 Make sure you open the sterile packages from the handle end.

Stage 4. Sterilizing your chosen growth media

Sterilize the growth medium, normally bought as a powder, as soon as it has been made up. Mix the medium as instructed on the packet, then transfer it into sterilized jars, using enough to cover the bottom to a depth of 1-1.5cm. Jam jars are good as they have a wide neck, and when it comes to sowing the seeds this gives you more room to manoeuvre, whereas a narrow-necked jar makes it difficult to manipulate seeds and seedlings at the bottom of the jar.

Sterilizing the medium can easily be done using a domestic pressure cooker. (In a laboratory this would be done with an autoclave, but a pressure cooker is effectively the same thing. It is possible to buy a laboratory autoclave, new or refurbished, but these are much more expensive than a pressure cooker.) Do not sterilize the medium in an oven, as it is too slow. Also, simply boiling the jars will not guarantee sterility. To ensure the medium is sterile, heat it at 121°C for 20 minutes.

Keep the jar lids a little loose during the sterilization process, with a square of aluminium foil over the loose lid to protect the contents until it is cool enough to screw the lid down securely. If the lids are screwed down too soon after sterilization, a partial vacuum will form in the jar, making it difficult to open with any control, and the resulting inrush of air can take contaminants into the jar.

Types of growth media

There are numerous types of media available for growing seed in culture, and they look more like soluble plant food than soil. Many were originally designed for germinating and growing tropical orchid species, while some were designed for different crop plants altogether. Whereas tropical orchids tend to be calcifuge, growing on acid soils without the presence of calcium, most of our native orchid species are calcicole - happy to grow on alkaline and chalky soils. But these commercial growth media for tropical orchids are still useful for our species:

- Knudson C
- Malmgren
- Phytamax
- Murashige and Skoog
- Mitra

The mixtures vary only by small amounts, but this can make a difference to the efficiency of seed germination. We have found Phytamax to be particularly good. In some cases the composition of the media is difficult to determine, as it is commercially sensitive, but those above have been clearly defined in academic papers over the years, and the media are reproducible from those publications, as a complete list of the contents was given.

Although it is possible to make up your own medium, this requires an accurate balance, some knowledge of chemistry, and access to a laboratory chemical supplier. It is much easier to use a modern commercial product, as they have a balanced salt content and a balanced acid/base composition (pH). All of the above products are available from the suppliers listed in Resources.

Whichever medium you choose, make sure it has agar in the recipe. If not, add it as 4g per 100ml of medium. This will ensure the growth medium sets in the jars, providing a solid surface for the seeds to sit on while they germinate.

If you feel more adventurous, try using recognized additives to enhance the growth of your seedlings. One of the regularly used additives is banana powder. Adding this at a rate of 5 per cent by weight will act as an efficient supplement.

> *There are numerous types of media available for growing seed in culture, and they look more like soluble plant food than soil.*

Stage 5. Sterilizing the seed

Once orchid seeds have been shed they pick up all sorts of contaminants from the environment. We get rid of these by sterilizing the seed and it is the outside of the seed that is treated and sterilized. Work in thin rubber gloves when setting up seed, because the outside of the glove can be sterilized easily while you are wearing them - use the methylated-spirits-and-water mix described in Stage 3 (see page 101).

The method of sterilizing seed depends on whether the seed was collected from pods in the green or from ripe pods.

Seed from green pods

(Green pods in this context means the first unripe pod above a pod that has started shedding seed.) The seed pod should have a complete and undamaged skin, so you can assume the inside of the pod is sterile. If the coat has been breached, discard the pod as it is likely to be contaminated.

The seed pod is best sterilized by using a thin domestic chlorine bleach, which can be bought as 'thin bleach' (do not use thick bleach). Remove all leftover flower and stalk remnants, then dip the pod into the bleach solution for approximately 10 minutes - the time needed to kill fungal spores. Now rinse the pod thoroughly in sterile water: ordinary tap water that has been autoclaved is best for this, but bottled water can be used (non-sparkling, of course). Use a good-quality, sterile, sharp blade to cut the pod open, gently scrape out the seeds with a sterilized spatula, and put them directly on to the sterile growth medium in a jar that you sterilized earlier. If there are a lot of seeds you may need to divide them between two jars.

> *Orchid seeds are relatively tough, but once they are on their growth medium, if they have any fungal spores with them they will be lost.*

and bottles. There is no need to sterilize the tissue paper before use, because it will be sterilized along with the seeds.

Alternatively, cut open an unused teabag and empty it. You now have a ready-made receptacle for about 500 seeds. The teabag can be simply dumped into your bleach and stirred gently to ensure the seeds are wet inside. Unless you have a lot of seed with which to experiment, err on the safe side and keep them in bleach for the longer time of 20 minutes.

Orchid seeds are relatively tough, but once they are on their growth medium, if they have any fungal spores with them they will be lost. Once sterilized, repeat the rinsing instructions in sterile water as for seeds from green pods (see page 103), then open the teabag or tissue package and scrape out the seeds, all with sterilized instruments, so that they can be transferred directly on to the growth medium.

Traditional method (seed from ripe pods)

The usual, and in some ways the easiest, method of sterilizing seed involves handling dry seed. Before starting, make sure the seed is viable, with a clear visible embryo within the testa (see box on page 97). Discard any duds. There are many versions of this method but they all require the seeds to be in a bleach solution for between 12 and 20 minutes.

Because the seeds are so small, some will get lost in the process of dry seed sterilization - either washed away or lodged in the equipment. There are two ways to minimize losses. Wrap your seeds in tissue paper before sterilizing them with the bleach. This keeps them all together and reduces the chance of them floating away or getting stuck to the inside of jars

Stage 6. Germinating the seed

Seeds of northern terrestrial orchid species normally only germinate in the dark. As soon as you have set up the seeds in culture, wrap the jars in aluminium foil to block out all the light. Label each jar carefully because the seedlings will all look the same, and without accurate labelling you won't be able to identify the species until it flowers.

Do not keep the jars anywhere too warm. These are outdoor species, and high temperatures will impede their germination and subsequent development. The temperature should not exceed 20°C, so a cool room works well. However, don't allow the temperature to drop below zero. Freezing won't harm the seeds, but it will make the growth medium separate and become useless. Many native orchid species will even germinate if the original sowing is kept in the refrigerator, though this is not recommended because of the danger to the growth medium.

After three days, unwrap the cultures and check for bacterial or fungal growth. When the seeds start to germinate they change colour from their original brown (unless they are Twayblades, which have white seeds) to a lighter shade. This is the first visible sign of germination. The seed is forming a protocorm (see Chapter 2, Figure 2.9, page 39) and will send out root hairs from the bundle of developing cells. Patience is required at this stage, as the seeds take from several weeks to several months to germinate, depending on conditions and the species.

Once the protocorms have started growing and can be clearly differentiated from each other, keep a close eye on their development, so that when they produce discernible roots or shoots they can be moved to new jars at a much lower density, still in strictly sterile conditions. At this stage the plants should still be kept in the dark until a distinct leaf shoot starts to appear. This takes anything from a month, for Common Spotted Orchids, to two years for Butterfly Orchids.

Because the young plants are growing in the dark, they will not produce chlorophyll and so will not be green. For most plants this would be a disadvantage, but these plants are growing on a completely defined medium, so they do not need to photosynthesize to produce sugars. However, they will be respiring, and producing carbon dioxide, which will slowly acidify the medium and the atmosphere in the jar. So as soon as distinct shoots are visible and the seedlings begin to look like plants, unwrap them to provide light, but do not touch the lids as you

Figure 5.10 Orchid seedlings ready for removal and transplantation.

need to maintain sterility. Great patience is needed with some species: four years is not unusual for Twayblades, while Common Spotted and Marsh Orchids may only take eight months.

Opening them to light enables the shoots to green up ready for the next stage - transplanting the seedlings into compost. It is important to green up the plants before transplanting them into pots, as they will need to be able to support themselves as soon as they are transplanted. The nascent plants have a shoot that has greened (Fig. 5.10), and a root. These rootlets need not be extensive, but they do have to be sufficient to stop the plant from dehydrating. Plants grown in sterile culture tend to have thin cuticles (the waterproof surface of the leaves and shoots), because they are in an environment where there is 100 per cent humidity and no air currents. They are delicate and very susceptible to dehydration and attack by pathogens, so make sure they are as robust as possible, with good roots and shoots (Fig. 5.11), before moving them into pots.

Figure 5.11 Green-winged Orchid seedling just about to be moved into a pot. The roots are very delicate but it can be handled quite easily with care. This seedling is a year old.

Figure 5.12 The seedlings need careful nurturing when first planted out.

Stage 7. Transplanting seedlings into pots

When to move your plants from sterile culture into pots depends very much on the species and time of year. If the plants are not strong enough to cope, they will fall over because of either damping off or dehydration.

Damping off is associated with fungal pathogens, such as *Phytophthora* and *Pythium*. The resulting disease takes its colloquial name from the way in which it attacks seedlings at the base, where they enter the soil. If the seedling has a thin cuticle and the atmosphere is both still and humid, the fungus will infect the plant and cause it to wilt. While damping off is caused by high humidity and still air, the newly potted orchids will be just as badly affected by dehydration if the air is breezy and dry. It is important, therefore, to balance the watering and ventilation carefully for the first few days after transplanting.

Often, just two or three days out of direct sunlight in a well-ventilated position will be enough to give the young plant time to acclimatize to its new conditions. Once established in

its pot, it can be treated like any other plant seedling. The potting compost to use will vary from species to species, though in truth it isn't necessary to be very specific. A good base is John Innes No. 2 with added garden lime (see the discussion of composts in Chapter 4, page 86 ['Choosing composts']).

The young plants then need to grow on in their pots (Fig. 5.12) before they are strong and settled enough to be planted out in their final positions, either in containers or naturalized in

Figure 5.13 After a year or two, the seedlings will have grown into robust and healthy plants, like this young Common Spotted Orchid.

the garden. For some species, such as Common Spotted Orchids, this process may take a year (Fig. 5.13); for others it is likely to be longer – for example, Pyramidal Orchids may take nearer to two years. When you decide the plants are ready, be very careful when planting out. The roots are both long and delicate, as can be seen in Figures 5.14 and 5.15 and it is very easy to damage them. See Chapter 4, page 78, for advice on planting out your orchids with minimal disturbance.

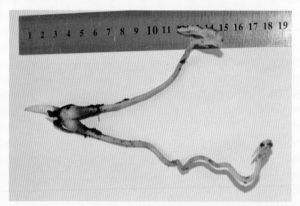

Figure 5.14 A three-year-old Common Spotted Orchid, already with very long roots. This was grown from seed using specialist techniques and has been in a pot for two years. The very long roots are why native orchids are difficult to transplant.

Figure 5.15 Although orchid roots seem bare, these of the Common Twayblade in close-up show the layer of fine root hairs through which water and nutrients are absorbed.

IN SUMMARY

Raising orchids from seed in culture requires great care and attention to detail, but the results are extremely rewarding. When collecting seed, do so responsibly, taking it only from abundant plants and common species. Dry seed can be stored for over a year.

You will need to purchase specialist growth media and organize a dedicated area to work in, sterilizing all equipment and materials, to ensure that the seed culture does not get contaminated. Some patience is required in the early stages of growth, but once the seedlings have both roots and shoots, they can be potted up to grow on into sturdy plants.

When you first start raising orchids from seed, begin with one of the easier native species. Most of the genus *Dactylorhiza* fall into this category. This includes the Common Spotted Orchid, the Heath Spotted Orchid and the Northern and Southern Marsh Orchids. Whichever species you start with, when your first plant raised from seed is finally established and flowering, you can be justly proud of your achievement - you are a practical conservationist.

Chapter Six

PESTS
and
DISEASES

Even wild plants have pests and diseases. Normally these go unnoticed and unrecorded, lost in a field of crop vegetables. When you grow plants in your garden, though, you can easily spot those that are not thriving and seem to have lost their sparkle. The sorts of pests and diseases you will have to deal with will depend to some extent on how you grow your orchids. For example, plants grown as single species in containers will be most vulnerable. By contrast, the most robust environment for orchids is a mixed meadow, where they are protected by the many different species surrounding them in a balanced and stable ecosystem.

Opposite: Broad-leaved Helleborine (*Epipactis helleborine*) with bramble (*Rubus fruticosus* agg.) and herb robert (*Geranium robertianum*). Hedgerow in early August.

> *Slugs and snails can destroy seedlings overnight and cause considerable damage to fully grown plants.*

Orchids are affected by the same pests that affect any garden plants. Birds and mammals are unlikely to cause much damage, but smaller pests can do more harm than might be apparent at first sight, because they can leave the plant vulnerable to disease. For instance, slug or snail damage can create an entry point for bacterial infections, while aphids and mites can spread viral diseases.

Although orchids need a symbiotic fungus to aid seed germination, they are just as susceptible to fungal or bacterial disease as any other plants. In fact certain diseases are specific to orchids and can affect whole populations in a single season, killing almost all the plants. Soil-borne diseases are more difficult to control than airborne ones, as the infectious organism is a resident part of the environment. Infections brought in by pests are best controlled by controlling the population of the pest, rather than trying to treat the disease itself.

That said, the general principle of organic gardening is that in a healthy and balanced system, pests and diseases will be kept in check by natural predators and by the plants' own defences. Think twice before taking drastic action against any garden foe, especially action involving toxic chemicals. Consider the ecological implications for your garden and the wider environment, in particular for wildlife.

BIRDS AND LARGE ANIMALS

Problems with wild animals and birds are not so common in urban gardens, but can be quite significant in suburban and country areas. We would encourage tolerance here, at least in the case of less common garden visitors such as badgers, which can cause damage by digging. Deer, especially muntjac, like orchid flowers and you can tell they have been in action as the flowers get nipped off but the stem is left standing. While this can be amusing once or twice, the novelty does wear off.

Smaller mammals such as squirrels, moles and rabbits are a nuisance because of their digging, but are unlikely to be targeting the plants themselves. On the other hand, mice might dig up orchids with pseudobulbs or tubers for food in severe winters. Birds, such as magpies and jays, also dig plants out of pots when looking for grubs underneath or seeking bulbs to eat. If bird and animal damage becomes an annoyance, the easiest way to protect the plants is to put a piece of wire or plastic netting over them.

SLUGS AND SNAILS

Slugs and snails can destroy seedlings overnight and cause considerable damage to fully grown plants. Slugs in particular are indiscriminate browsers, and once in the secluded confines of a pot they are protected against their natural predators and have little else to

How to grow NATIVE ORCHIDS in gardens large and small

Figure 6.1 Slug eggs, laid in a flowerpot. The plant roots can be seen with the eggs.

eat than your plant. The pot also provides a sheltered spot to lay their eggs (Fig. 6.1).

Slugs often use the bottom of flowerpots as daytime shelter, so check underneath pots for them. They hide out in damp, dark places by day, so it's fairly easy to trap them by placing upside-down dishes on the ground, lifting them later to reveal the slugs. Some people swear by upside-down half-grapefruit skins. Often, 'hunting' the slugs is more than half the battle in controlling them. Put them in the compost bin if you cannot bear to kill them.

Copper has been shown to be an effective barrier against slugs, and a ring of copper tape around a container will act as a deterrent, as will copper feet on any racking that you keep your plants on. A ring of Vaseline smeared around the rim of a pot is another option; for added effect, mix salt into it. However, this washes off with rain and needs to be reapplied.

A recent development in biological slug control uses a microscopic nematode called *Phasmarhabditis hermaphrodita*, which is grown in culture with a bacterium, *Moraxella osloensis*. This bacterium infects the nematode, which then parasitizes and eventually kills the slug. The solution is watered on to the garden, providing slug control for about six weeks. Not all slugs are equally affected, but the smaller species, which cause most damage, can be controlled.

Avoid using slug pellets containing metaldehyde, which is metabolized by the slug and kills it. Although coloured to discourage birds and flavoured to discourage consumption by larger animals like hedgehogs, dogs and cats, they represent a risk to wildlife. They may also be no more effective than other more benign approaches, as their effectiveness is dependent on all manner of things, including the weather.

WOODLICE

Woodlice like to eat orchid greenery, but usually this is only a problem in greenhouses and conservatories, where their food is limited to what is being grown there (Figure 6.2). They are detritus feeders, eating decaying vegetable matter (and rotting wood), but they will use pots as shelter, and that's when they may eat the soft parts of roots and shoots. Woodlice are

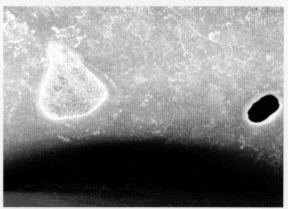
Figure 6.2 Leaf damage caused by woodlice, in this case on the leaf of a Moth Orchid.

definitely to be tolerated rather than treated as pests, but if you are bothered by them, put down a cut apple or potato to attract them away from your orchids; otherwise, regard them as neighbours.

APHIDS

Aphids, which include the greenfly and black-fly, can cause considerable harm to orchids, as they are indiscriminate feeders. I have frequently found them overwintering on potted hardy orchids, where they seem quite happy to sit the season out (Fig 6.3). They are all sap suckers, and spread diseases by direct puncture of the plant's vascular system.

The amount of damage aphids do will depend on the size and age of the plants. They are more likely to cause problems to small plants in pots in a cold frame or conservatory than to established plants in the garden.

Small plants can be set back, though rarely killed, by aphid infestations (Fig. 6.4). Use a soap solution: if you have time, brush the solution on, as this will lift many of the aphids from the plant. If you find a lot of them on your plants under cover, you can use an insecticide to control them, but insecticides should not be used outside. The spray may drift and kill more insects than the one you are targeting, and insecticides can cause a damaging ecological imbalance. Even if you use a watering can, the insecticide may remain at soil level. Remember that aphids have natural predators in the garden - ladybirds, hoverfly larvae and lacewing larvae - which are of great value to the gardener.

Many aphids have a happy symbiotic relationship with ants, which can often be seen roaming among the aphids on the plants, keeping predators away and feeding on the

Figure 6.3 A single aphid overwintering on a Pyramidal Orchid seedling. The plant is two years old.

Figure 6.4 An infestation of aphids on a seedling orchid. This level of aphids can cause problems to such a small plant.

sugar-laden liquid that the aphids exude. So unless the problem is severe, allow the aphids to stay, otherwise you risk damaging the ant colony as well.

MITES

The glasshouse red spider mite, *Tetranychus urticae*, is the mite pest you are most likely to come across on your plants. It is a tiny arachnid, less than 0.5mm long. Normally considered greenhouse pests, they can cause problems to

Marsh Helleborine (*Epipactis palustris*).

outdoor plants if the weather is warm and dry. Leaf mottling is the primary symptom, becoming severe as infestation increases. Although small, the mites' bright red colour makes them easy to spot. If the infestation is very large, you can see what is easily mistaken for a spider's web, but in fact it's a web made up of chaotic thread production by large numbers of spider mites.

Control by hand by physically removing them. You can use an insecticide indoors, but biological control using *Phytoseiulus persimilis,* an arachnid barely larger than the mite, is a better method. Or make life uncomfortable for the mites with cool, damp conditions. If the mites have affected plants outside, remember that a turn to cold, wet weather will solve the problem.

MEALY BUGS AND SCALE INSECTS

Mealy bugs aren't generally a nuisance, except in the greenhouse or conservatory, or occasionally in pots under cover in cold frames. There are about 25 nuisance species in Northern Europe, all looking like bumps or nodules on the underside of leaves. This bump is the insect's protective carapace, which it clamps down to the leaf surface when not moving about sucking the sap. In a greenhouse, they are easily controlled by a mixture of methylated spirits and detergent. Outdoors, ladybirds are their natural predators.

You can spot scale insects on leaves as limpet-like structures (Fig. 6.5), which is the insect more or less clamped to the leaf by its legs. The insects are very firmly attached and well protected, so they are difficult to get rid of without the use of a systemic insecticide.

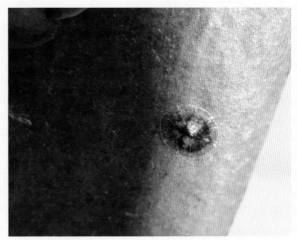

Figure 6.5 Scale insect on an orchid leaf. Note the limpet-like appearance.

FUNGAL DISEASES

Fungal diseases of orchids pose a very specific problem for growers hoping to develop a colony or just a small group of naturalized plants. Because all new orchid seedlings that appear naturally have germinated with a symbiotic fungus, using a fungicide could kill this symbiotic fungus as well as the fungal disease.

One of the first symptoms of fungal infections on leaves is anthracnose, a discolouration and disfigurement of the leaves (Figs 6.6 and 6.7). There are many different fungal causes of anthracnose, such as *Botrytis*, a problem on commercial vines. On your orchids, this mould will invade areas of leaf damage and can stop the plant from growing and flowering for the season, so although it may not die, it will be severely weakened. (This is a good reason for making sure growth has ceased before making an autumn meadow cut: see Chapter 7, page 130).

Many of the fungi that cause problems are not necessarily pathogens but are often speculative invaders of damaged tissue, which

Figure 6.6 The signs of disease on a Common Spotted Orchid leaf. This discolouration and disfiguration is referred to as anthracnose.

Figure 6.7 Marsh Helleborine leaves showing signs of anthracnose.

weakens the plant. This is why slug damage is particularly harmful – not only does it look unsightly but it can also be the entry point for an infectious organism that may kill the plant.

While some species of the fungus *Rhizoctonia* are pathogens, many are known to be orchid symbionts, essential for natural seed germination, so the situation can become complicated.

It *is* possible to treat your plants with a fungicide, but it will put back the natural germination of seeds in the soil and can easily disrupt the ecosystem. Where fungicide has been used in the past, it can persist. If establishing an orchid colony in an orchard is slower than expected, fungicide may have been used and it is worth digging out the area and replacing the soil before replanting your orchids.

Cladosporium orchidis

Cladosporium orchidis is a fungal species that invades orchid colonies and almost wipes them out. As its name implies, it is a disease almost exclusively of orchids, most devastating in colonies of *Dactylorhiza*. This may be because some

Dactylorhiza species – for example, the Common Spotted and Marsh Orchids (Fig. 6.8) – form quite dense colonies, so transmission between plants is easier.

The infection starts as brown spots, which develop and spread, resulting in prematurely

Figure 6.8 The start of an infection by *Cladosporium orchidis* on a Southern Marsh Orchid growing in a damp meadow. The colony was severely damaged by this infection, producing no flowers for several years.

dead foliage and a weakened plant. It does not seem to be systemic, as plants will try to regrow the following year. Susceptibility also varies considerably among plants within a colony, so if you are growing these orchids in your garden, it's wise to obtain plants from different seed sources, which a competent grower will be able to organize for you.

The disease is encouraged by warm weather in spring followed by cold and wet weather. The precocious early growth due to the warm weather is then damaged by the harsh weather, resulting in lesions that can let in infectious spores. This is likely to become a more common problem in Northern Europe as global warming brings changes to our seasons. *Cladosporium orchidis* is a normal soil-borne fungus, so it is unclear why it suddenly becomes active in orchid colonies, but entry of the disease is probably linked with physical damage.

Mitigate against the weather by moving container grown plants under shelter to minimize physical damage from harsh conditions. Using a fungicide on plants in pots will reduce the seed set around the plants, but is less of a concern than using it in a naturalized colony. Treat affected plants by removing the infected leaves, and accept that they will miss a year's growth and flowers. This is a small price to pay for the long-term survival of your orchids, which can live for many years. Indeed as more people grow these amazing plants in controlled conditions, we are learning that they will live for 10 years or more unless attacked by disease. Bee Orchids, once thought to be monocarpic (flowering once, then dying), can flower for over 20 years. Early Purple Orchids have been recorded flowering for more than a dozen years.

BACTERIAL DISEASES

Although fungal disease is the main problem that wild populations of orchids have to contend with, rot diseases caused by bacterial infections can also occur. These start at ground level, attacking the root and tuber (Fig 6.9), or they can start and spread from spots on the leaves. If the problem starts with the tuber, then it may never be obvious what has happened, as the plant will simply disappear. These infections are often started by physical damage from slugs or snails. If your orchids are struggling to grow, this is when they are at risk of becoming infected.

The most common cause of rot is being too wet. If one of your plants shows signs of rot, check whether it is waterlogged and take steps to halt the process. For plants in pots, it is best to repot them, as waterlogging compacts compost. No matter whether it is a high- or low-organic mix, compost that has been waterlogged for any length of time will compact when it dries out.

Avoiding wet conditions is the only real method of controlling bacterial infections in orchids. If just one plant in a group in a pot is

Figure 6.9 Bacterial damage starting at ground level will manifest by the leaves collapsing to the ground as the infection destroys the leaf support.

infected, remove it and repot the remaining plants to prevent further infection.

Most of the knowledge of bacterial orchid problems stems from work on tropical varieties, where there is commercial pressure to control disease. However, these plants are nearly always cultivated under glass, in an artificial world. Growing orchids in your garden, whether in pots, flower beds or naturalized, is different. They are part of a perpetuating ecosystem where diseases may occur, but not usually severely enough to cause major problems. Unless you are growing for show, every single leaf doesn't need to be perfect, and a little spotting occurs quite naturally and should not be regarded as a problem. Bacterial infections can come and go in an orchid community, and while they may cause the death of individual plants, this does not necessarily mean the end of the population.

VIRAL DISEASES

Viral diseases of orchids are of considerable significance to commercial growers, as they are quite common and cause unwanted changes to otherwise healthy plants. Consequently most of the research on such diseases has been done on tropical species.

Viral infections are often long term and virtually benign as far as the orchid is concerned. They are transmitted by insects, such as aphids, and the plant carries the infection without being killed by it. However, the infections pose a problem for commercial growers, as often they first manifest in the flower, in what is called a colour break - a disruption to the continuous colour. Colour breaks are encouraged in plants such as tulips in order to create intricate patterns.

Despite the dedication to this subject in tropical orchid species, viral infections of British and Irish native orchids are not well researched. However, it is likely that most are also long term and benign.

What we *do* know is that the primary, and sometimes only, symptom of viral infection in our native species is unexpected yellowing of the leaves. This is sometimes seen in Butterfly Orchids, and the discolouration can start quite early in the year. In terms of treatment, unless the infection is severe, it is best to do nothing; otherwise dispose of the plant and its compost. Magnesium deficiency also causes yellowing of leaves, so if you think you have a virus problem, check your soil for mineral deficiencies first.

IN SUMMARY

Pests and diseases are a normal part of any ecosystem, and as far as possible should be accepted as part of nature. The benefits of attracting a wider range of wildlife with naturalized and diverse planting should far outweigh any satisfaction gained from controlling your garden with the use of herbicides and insecticides. Growing orchids in your garden makes a statement that you care about the environment.

If a specific pest increases to a level that becomes a problem, there are ways of alleviating the situation. Most diseases are transient in a well-balanced garden and do not need to be treated aggressively. Enjoy your plants: some may not last as well as others, but with a healthy ecosystem you will have an enduring population of orchids that will repay you for your care.

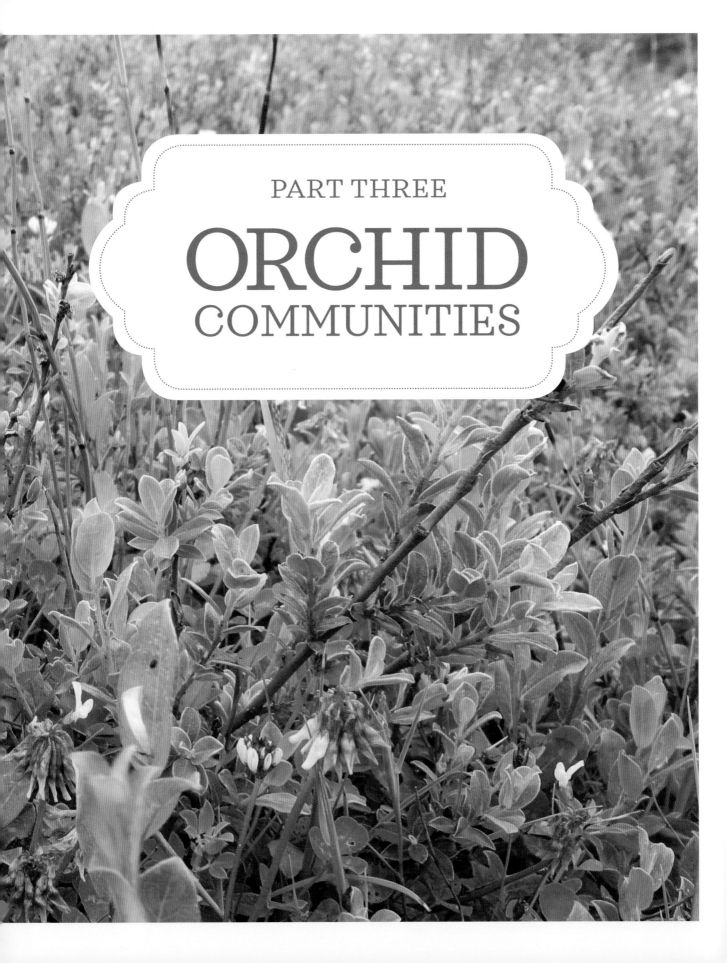

PART THREE

ORCHID
COMMUNITIES

Chapter Seven

Creating a
GARDEN
meadow

For many, the attraction of growing native orchids lies in creating a scene of orchids in one of their natural habitats, such as grassland. A semi-wild garden meadow is one of the easiest orchid habitats to create, and can be done on any scale. It's possible to turn a lawn or even a patch of bare earth or weeds into a meadow of wild flowers and beautiful native orchids, as pictured on pages 122 (Fig. 7.1) and 123 (Fig. 7.2). This chapter explains how to create your own orchid meadow - a place of contemplation and a haven for biodiversity. Orchid flowers are very attractive to bees and butterflies, so if you develop a plot where your orchids can grow to their full potential, other wildlife will follow.

Opposite: Green-winged Orchid (*Anacamptis morio*) with primrose (*Primula vulgaris*) and glaucous sedge (*Carex flacca*). Meadow in early May.

Figure 7.1 An established meadow with Green-winged Orchids and Common Spotted Orchids.

All our meadows have to be maintained, or they will start to grow scrub and eventually trees; and in the British climate, lowland areas eventually return to broadleaved woodland. The good news is that maintenance of a garden meadow, whether large or small, is a lot less effort than having to cut a lawn every week or so. All that's needed is an annual cut at the end of the growing season, making sure that seeds from the annual plants, such as yellow rattle, are not removed.

LAWN TREATMENTS

If you are turning an existing lawn into a garden meadow, the first thing to consider is whether the lawn has been treated with 'weed and feed'. Both these processes are bad news for a nascent meadow. The weedkiller part usually refers to herbicides, aimed at broadleaved weeds like dandelions and plantains. In the past, this herbicide would have been 2,4-Dichlorophen-oxyacetic acid or 2,4,5-Trichlorophenoxyacetic acid. Of these, 2,4,5-T is no longer used, but 2,4-D acid is still widely found in combination with fertilizers designed to promote grass growth. Although these hormone weedkillers do not directly harm orchids you plant, the associated changes in soil fertility from using these mixtures will cause problems. The ferti-lizer content causes increased growth in all the plants, but orchids are relatively slow-growing

Figure 7.2 Common Spotted Orchids are an attractive and reliable choice for a meadow.

so they tend to get swamped by the fast, luxuriant growth of grasses. Given time, these treatments should not cause any permanent damage to a garden meadow, as they will be gradually removed by soil microbes and by cutting and removing the grass.

A few of the weedkillers that are occasionally used to clear grasses and scrub, like glyphosate, do not persist in the soil for as long as the hormone weedkillers, so these may cause less of a long-term problem in developing a meadow. Some even suggest using one of the glyphosate-based herbicides to eradicate all plants before setting up a meadow plot, but this draconian method is not one we would recommend. If the development of a meadow is done gently and with care, the constant change every year as the balance between species alters will be a delight and is as much a pleasure as the mature meadow will be. Even when the meadow is mature, changes will be seen, with comings and goings of all manner of wildlife.

If your plot has been treated with fertilizer or has fertile soil, you will need to reduce its fertility, otherwise excessive growth of grass will swamp everything else. For larger areas, dig up and remove the topsoil to reveal the subsoil, or turn the ground so that the subsoil comes to the top. For smaller areas, it's best to cut and remove the grass, as this will gradually remove the excess nutrients from the soil.

If you have a lawn that has never been

treated with chemical weedkiller or fertilizer, things couldn't be better for starting a small garden meadow. The lovely thing about this process is that it doesn't have to be set in stone. The meadow area can be made bigger or smaller as you choose. Digging an edge or putting in artificial edging is unnecessary and would detract from the overall feel of the garden meadow. It should be a free-form area in both size and shape.

CREATING YOUR MEADOW

The best time to start your meadow is early spring. You can start later in the growing season, but it may be a little ragged in the first year. A start in autumn will not give quick results.

If you are starting with a mown lawn, decide how much of it you wish to turn over to meadow, and leave that area uncut next time you mow. The same applies to an unkempt area of long grass, but check there are no unwanted plants beginning to grow, such as brambles, which can be removed by hand at this stage. Then get out the lawn mower (see box on page 130) and cut the area around your meadow area so that it is clearly defined (Figs 7.3-7.5).

If the area has no existing grass, you're in the ideal position of sowing the patch with wild-flower seed directly. If you are starting with a grassy area, just gently rake the seed into the grass: germination may be slightly reduced compared with bare soil, but this will quickly balance in following years. Don't bother with grass seed on bare soil, as grasses will arrive on their own. Put in a mix of annual and perennial wild-flower seeds (see pages 126-128) to maintain a balance within the meadow area until your patch is established. Seed is best spread at

Figure 7.3 An uncut garden plot. The area around the apple tree has been chosen for conversion to meadow.

Figure 7.4 The garden plot marked out by using the lawn mower. It has just been left to grow for a few weeks.

Figure 7.5 The meadow plot some weeks later, now with a path cut through it.

a density of about 1.5g per square metre. Sowing should be as mixed as possible, so that you don't have blocks of single species. Once you have sown your wild-flower seed, it's time to plant the orchids.

When planting your orchids, be careful not to damage the roots, and make sure they are planted deep enough so they don't dry out in the early days while they establish. Full details about the best way to plant can be found in Chapter 4.

CHOOSING YOUR ORCHIDS

Give careful thought to the choice of orchid species to include in your meadow. This will depend not only on the species' preferred growing conditions but also on their annual flowering and growth cycles. The latter is important because you will be cutting the meadow once a year, and will want to ensure that the timing of this cut is not detrimental to any of your orchids, whether by curtailing their growth or by preventing them from setting seed. This is discussed on page 130.

Established orchids are generally unfussy and some species can be remarkably flexible about soil type. The Pyramidal Orchid is an example of this: we have seen it growing in the deep shade of a wood and also on heavy clay. As a rule, however, choosing species that prefer a similar soil type is the best way to produce a good sustainable population. The following species are suitable for an open meadow. They are all described in detail in Chapter 3, along with their preferred soil conditions.

- Bee Orchid
- Chalk Fragrant Orchid
- Common Spotted Orchid
- Common Twayblade

> *Established orchids are generally unfussy and some species can be remarkably flexible about soil type.*

- Greater Butterfly Orchid
- Green-winged Orchid
- Heath Spotted Orchid
- Northern Marsh Orchid
- Pyramidal Orchid
- Southern Marsh Orchid

Some of these species, such as the Marsh Orchids, do best in areas that are damp. If you have a sloping area and the bottom of the slope stays damp throughout the summer, this will be ideal for them.

MEADOW PLANTS TO INCLUDE WITH YOUR ORCHIDS

In addition to orchids in your garden meadow, include other wild flowers and meadow plants to enhance its biodiversity and colour.

In your plot, include 'nature's lawnmower', yellow rattle (Fig. 7.6), which is partially parasitic on various species of grass. You will find

Figure 7.6 Yellow rattle, 'nature's lawnmower', is an important species to include in a wild-flower meadow.

Resources. Besides yellow rattle, which is an annual, these would include perennials such as the following.

Perennials

Cowslip. This tall cousin of the primrose needs no introduction. It prefers the open sunshine of a meadow and can cope with the longer grass found there.

Devil's-bit scabious (Fig. 7.7) and **field scabious**. These two flowers are very similar in appearance, with field scabious preferring conditions a bit drier than devil's-bit scabious. Both seem to prefer chalky soil, but can be grown in soils that are not strongly acid.

Common knapweed (Fig. 7.8) and **greater knapweed** (Fig. 7.9). These two species are very similar, both having a thistle-like flower without the spiky foliage of a thistle. Greater knapweed is a good indicator of a calcareous soil, while common knapweed takes its place everywhere else.

Hawkbits. There are a number of these to choose from, each one having a dandelion-like flower, often tall and on branched stems.

Meadow buttercup (Fig. 7.10). The flowers of this buttercup can be up to 25mm across and are easily seen, as they stand tall, at 60cm or more high. Although some buttercups are annual, this tall species is a perennial.

Mouse-ear hawkweed. This plant has a dandelion-like flower but also a creeping root, so it can form small mats. This habit is unlikely to be a problem in a varied meadow setting, and the plant will form a lovely yellow backdrop early in the summer.

Ox-eye daisy. A lovely flower of open grassland, but easily swamped by tall and dense grass cover.

this annual flower in meadows that are intermittently grazed or cut at specific times of the year, but not where there is constant grazing by sheep. Be a little cautious when buying seed, as it loses its viability quickly and does best sown the same year as it is produced.

Wild-flower seed mixes sold for meadows tend to be biased towards tall flowers, so it can look decorative but artificial, and they have two disadvantages: first, because the seeds in the mix are unbalanced, the resulting show will not be self-sustaining; and second, there are usually very few, if any, perennial seeds in the mix. These mixes are useful for getting started and will give a short-term covering to a plot, but the result may be rather different from a naturally formed and evolved meadow.

To make your meadow special, choose your seed yourself, and include plants that would be regarded as weeds in the greens of the local golf course but are an essential part of a meadow. You should be able to get most of the plant seed you require from the suppliers listed in

Figure 7.7 Devil's-bit scabious is another wild flower very popular with insects, like this brimstone butterfly.

Figure 7.8 Common knapweed is a common perennial of grasslands and very popular with butterflies, such as this small skipper.

Figure 7.9 On chalky grassland you are more likely to find greater knapweed than common knapweed.

Figure 7.10 Meadow buttercup, a perennial species, is a mainstay of the traditional wild-flower meadow.

Red clover. Although quite a robust clover, this is most often to be found in grassland where the vegetation is not too tall. While closely related to vetches, it doesn't have grasping tendrils to scramble through thick vegetation. Red clover can also be white!

Ribwort plantain and **greater plantain.** These are very easily recognized, greater plantain being a common plant in garden lawns. Neither species has showy flowers, but their presence is a delight in the summer meadow.

Adding in various species of trefoils and

other hawkweeds will also benefit the plot. If you have a chalky soil, then greater knapweed can replace common knapweed, and small scabious can replace devil's-bit scabious if the chalk content becomes very high.

Annuals

Annual flowers for your meadow would include such plants as the following. You could use a seed mix as a basis here, as they are largely comprised of annual species.

When growing annual plants in your meadow, remember that they have to seed before you cut it in the autumn, or you will not have flowers coming up in the following year.

Black medick. This is a common plant of short grassland, and is a wild relative of the pea; the leaves and flowers being unmistakably pea-like. It can be mistaken for a clover, to which it is also closely related.

Cornflower (Fig. 7.11). is very closely related to the knapweeds, but is lighter and smaller.

Common poppy. This poppy is difficult to separate from the four or so other blood-red poppies that can be found in arable fields and meadows. Eventually common poppy and cornflower will die out naturally when there is a complete cover of perennials.

Yellow rattle. 'Nature's lawnmower' is the mainstay of grass control, as it is partially parasitic on various species of perennial grass.

There are also many species of annual grass that may appear in your meadow, such as:

- loose silky bent
- wild oat
- annual beard-grass
- and, of course, annual meadow grass.

A diversity of species

Vetches are always found in meadows as a wide range of species, both annual and perennial. All are in the pea family and have a pea-like flower and pods for seeds. Like peas, they tend to scramble through the vegetation, with prolific flowers.

The above lists are just a selection of plants that look good in a meadow. Don't forget the biennial flowers, such as ragwort (but see box opposite) and ploughman's spikenard. The idea is to complement the orchids in your garden with wild plants that would be expected to grow with them in a meadow. Have a look at a meadow in flower to see what you are aiming for.

MAINTAINING YOUR MEADOW

Once the area of your meadow is defined and you have planted your orchids and sown other meadow flowers, it should be maintained by cutting once a year.

Most of the plants that will arrive in your meadow over time will be easy to control by cutting if you don't want them. Similarly, if you do want to keep them, then careful timing of cutting can help them seed and develop. However,

Figure 7.11 The brilliant blue of cornflowers in a meadow are hard to beat.

Unwelcome plants

Although regular cutting will control annual weeds, the perennial weeds in your grass plot will persist with only one cut a year, unless they are hand-weeded. The following perennials are invasive, and should be removed as often as you can. Fortunately these plants are all quite recognizable and are easily controlled by hand (with gloves, in the case of some!).

- **Broad-leaved dock** grows to one metre in height and produces huge numbers of seeds. It is best weeded out by hand as soon as it is recognizable and before it puts down its taproot. It is not generally a problem in converted lawns, where it turns up rarely.

- **Thistles** of various types can appear, as the seed is easily blown on the wind. Some species are quite decorative, but they are generally best weeded out to keep the overall height of the meadow area lower.

- The same is true of **nettles**. They do best on nitrogen-enriched soils, which is one of the reasons they are so often seen around field edges and in areas of agricultural run-off.

- One of the invasive species that is almost guaranteed to turn up from time to time is the all-too-familiar **bramble**. As soon as this is seen, it should be removed. The reason for its ubiquitous presence is that birds spread the seeds in their droppings, so whenever they fall on fertile ground, a plant will grow, and before you know it there is a great prickly thicket.

- **Ragwort** (Fig. 7.12) may have a bearing on how you dispose of your meadow cuttings, as it is poisonous to livestock. If you are *quite sure* that you are not growing ragwort, then you can offer your hay as suitable for livestock feed. Ragwort is a very recognizable plant, often seen growing in paddocks as a result of overgrazing. It has a pleasant daisy-like flower and is important for wildlife, being a favoured food plant for cinnabar moths and their caterpillars. The caterpillar accumulates toxic and bitter-tasting substances from the ragwort, which makes it unpalatable to birds.

Figure 7.12 Ragwort is of value to various insects, especially the cinnabar moth. Here, the flowers are being enjoyed by a copper butterfly.

there are some species that shouldn't be allowed to get a foothold - see box on page 129.

It is important to remove the cut vegetation, but, unless it is a very late cut (that is, well into the autumn), you should leave the cut grass to dry before raking it up. This gives time for seeds from annual flowers to drop out of the seed pods so that they produce plants the next year.

There are two main reasons for removing the cut grass:

- If it is left to lie over winter, it will kill many of the less hardy plants that it covers, by starving them of light.
- Long-term husbandry. By removing the cuttings, you remove nutrients and this will slow down the grasses and other shallow-rooted plants, which in turn will reduce the amount of cutting required. On steeply sloping plots, vegetation tends to be thinner, so although it may not be quite so important to remove the clippings, it is still worth the effort.

WHEN TO CUT YOUR MEADOW

Some meadow flowers are annuals, so once they have a place in your meadow, they should be left to seed before any cutting is done. Timing will depend on the weather and your local climate, but by leaving the cut as late as possible into the autumn, you can be sure that seeds have set. If you don't let this happen, then in two years the annuals will more or less have disappeared and only the perennials will remain. But the perennials won't last for ever, so they also need to be left to seed

Similarly, if you want the orchids in your garden to propagate, cutting should be timed to coincide with them having shed their seeds. As we saw in Chapter 2, orchids have an annual

Which mower or cutting tool?

Cutting Paths

For cutting paths through the meadow area, there's a lot to be said for a cylinder mower, but this really isn't suitable for making the annual cut of the meadow itself. Our preference for paths is a hover mower. This lends itself to being manoeuvred around bends and corners, with no loss of cutting performance as you go slower to cut curves and edges accurately. It's best not to try and cut the pathways with a strimmer, as this will result in an uneven cut and a rather straggly appearance. It also takes considerable skill to be consistent in following an edge accurately each time. The last thing you want to do is inadvertently cut off the tops of flowers growing close to the edge of the path.

Figure 7.13 A traditional Austrian scythe can be used very effectively on a small plot.

How to grow NATIVE ORCHIDS in gardens large and small

Cutting a meadow

The three best tools for cutting a meadow are a scythe, strimmer and power scythe.

Scythes

There is no doubt that using a scythe is a very good and satisfying way of cutting an area of meadow, but it is strenuous. There are three basic types of scythe, if you include the single-handed sickle in this category.

The sickle is a back-breaking implement to use for any length of time. While its short handle and hacking blade make it easy to manipulate in scrub, it requires considerable skill to use in grass.

The sickle's larger relative, the scythe, also requires practice and skill to use, but it produces a much better finish. There are two types of full-sized scythes, the Anglo-American traditional scythe (weighing about 3kg) and the Austrian scythe (weighing about 1.8kg).

Strimmers

If you want the annual cut of your meadow to be easier, you may want to use a strimmer. These can be either electrically powered or, supported on a harness for balance, powered by a small petrol engine. Although the petrol-engined version is robust and portable (the favourite of local authorities), these have two major disadvantages: they are very noisy and very smelly.

Power scythes

The third device that is ideal for cutting a meadow, but really only if you have a large plot or one with woody scrub that needs clearing, is the power scythe (Fig. 7.14). It operates by having a blade of fingers sliding backwards and forwards across a static blade of similar fingers, in exactly the same way as an electric hair clipper works. These devices are all powered by petrol engines, and as a consequence are also noisy.

For the annual meadow cut, a substantial hover mower works well, but any collection box has to be removed first, and it does need to have a steel blade. These mowers are quite hard work because they need to be held up much of the time, and this also adds to the risk of accidents.

Figure 7.14 The power scythe, like this Lawnflite model, cuts long grass well and is easy to handle.

Figure 7.15 The Bee Orchid is one of our few native winter-green species.

cycle of growth, flowering and fruiting. There may be more flowers in some years than in others, but the timing of the flowering cycle will be largely the same. Seed production occurs about 6-8 weeks after the end of flowering. See Table 3.2 in Chapter 3 for flowering times for our recommended orchids. This depends a lot on the weather, which is why we give a wide range in the timings there.

Some authorities advocate two cuts a year, in autumn and in early spring. But anything carried out after January in a warm year risks causing damage to the newly growing orchid shoots and can take the early flower spikes off. If this happens, your orchids will not flower the same year, so to ensure minimal disruption, leave the cutting until autumn.

As explained in Chapter 2, our native orchids are of two types: winter dormant and winter green. Most of our species are winter dormant, but the time at which they become so varies, as does the earliest time of the autumn cut. With the exception of the Bee Orchid (Fig. 7.15), the Green-winged Orchid and the Pyramidal Orchid, all the species listed on page 125 ['Choosing your orchids'] are winter dormant.

Winter-dormant species generally flower around June and July, so cut from September through to February. If there is a risk of early growth and shoots above ground in unseasonably warm weather, it would be better to make the last cut of the season around Christmas. Helleborines, unlike other winter-dormant orchids, keep their green leaves until the first frosts, so should not be cut too soon (see Chapter 8, page 138 ['Planting and maintaining your orchard or glade']).

The winter-green species also flower around June and July, and after setting seed about six weeks later, they die back to ground level. From October onwards, they will start to produce new leaves and will then be vulnerable to damage, so cut the grass around September time, to avoid disturbance. Winter-green orchids are also vulnerable to physical damage by being walked on in winter, which is true for any plants that are frozen in the ground. While this will not kill them, it will put them back when they start to grow again in the spring. So treat your meadow plants with care, even at this time of year.

In summary, when deciding when to cut your meadow, there is a balance to be struck between the different needs of your orchids. The key points are:

- Wait until the end of the growing season, when your orchids and all the annual species have finished flowering and set seed.
- Confine the cutting as much as possible to the autumn months, since after December you risk damaging early-starters as well as winter-green species.
- If you have winter-green orchids, cut before October, and don't cut the meadow so short as to compromise these plants.

Meadow management for yellow rattle

As mentioned earlier, it is worth including yellow rattle in your meadow, as it will help to suppress vigorous grass growth. Rather than letting it look after itself, the best method of ensuring an annual growth of yellow rattle is to collect the seed before you cut the meadow and then re-seed it immediately afterwards. Seed is produced from mid-June to the end of July, so start collecting when the first seeds turn brown, and carry on until there are no more flowers coming out. The seed does best if it is raked into the base of any grass that is growing. It will germinate the following spring, generally in April.

If you don't manage to do this, don't worry – it will normally be quite all right just to cut the grass after the yellow rattle has set seed. But this plant is pivotal in controlling the grass, so any helping hand you can give it will be worthwhile.

IN SUMMARY

The first thing to do with your meadow is to enjoy it! Both you and your visitors will gravitate to your meadow, just to look at the flowers and listen to the insects.

When creating a garden meadow, take into account the previous treatment your lawn has had. The less weedkiller and fertilizer the better. Introduce your orchids and wild flowers with consideration for how they will grow together. Don't overcrowd the area when you first plant your meadow, and be patient - these meadows are not like flower borders, showing instant results, but will develop their own character over time, maturing into a beautiful semi-wild ecosystem where your orchids can flourish.

Yellow rattle will give some control of the grass, but an autumn cut will be required after the flowers have seeded. With a larger area this activity can become a party, as everyone likes messing about in a meadow and willing helpers are easy to find.

Chapter Eight

An ORCHID orchard or garden glade

Many of our native orchids grow wild in woodlands, adding a special charm to these habitats, and if you would like to create a similar scene in your garden, the effect will be truly rewarding. Perhaps you have a patch of garden with a few trees, or have a vision of creating a small orchard, with a carpet of orchids and other wild flowers beneath? If you have a shady edge or hedge, this can also become home to some of our loveliest wild orchids. This chapter describes how to establish one of these beautiful three-dimensional ecosystems. As soon as you plant a hedge or grow a tree, you are creating a safe haven above ground for birds, bats and insects.

Opposite: Southern Marsh Orchid (*Dactylorhiza praetermissa*) with Meadow Buttercup (*Ranunculus acris*) and Lady's Smock (*Cardamine pratensis*). Meadow in early June.

Figure 8.1 The Common Spotted Orchid is very tolerant of a range of conditions and will grow in light shade at the edge of trees.

TREES FOR AN ORCHID ORCHARD

If you are designing your orchid woodland from scratch, there's a good reason for opting for fruit trees rather than other tree species. If you are going to grow trees, why not produce an edible crop at the same time? Besides, apple and pear trees are lovely in themselves. They have wonderful flowers that shed petals like confetti and leaves that glisten with spring sunshine.

The common idea of an orchard is just a field full of fruit trees, but there's much more to it than that. It is important to match the type of tree to your plot, as not all fruit trees are suitable for the garden.

When growing apples, pears and plums, the variety is not so important as the rootstock, which mainly determines the eventual height of the tree. Particularly in the case of apple trees, there are many options available, including dwarfing and semi-dwarfing rootstocks (Fig. 8.2). Trees on dwarfing rootstocks can be planted about 3m apart, which will give a good amount of light for plants growing underneath. If you have enough space, you can plant your orchard with full-sized trees (Fig. 8.3). The usual recommended planting distance for these is up to 6m apart, though this is for the benefit of fruit production and can be considerably reduced to suit the space available. Whether you plant small or larger trees, the underplanting with both orchids and other wild flowers is the same.

For full-sized fruit trees, it is normal practice to prune so that the first branch comes off the trunk at about 1.5-2m above the ground. This provides branches low enough to make fruit picking easy, but not so low that they cause drip problems for the plants underneath. Also, at that height you can take a power mower right

In a natural deciduous woodland, the trees are separated by fairly large distances and quite a bit of light hits the woodland floor. In the spring, before leaf growth gets under way, a large number of understorey flowers will grow, including bluebells and a number of woodland orchids. (And not only the obvious woodland species - see Fig. 8.1). While some species are more tolerant of greater shade, and a few are happy in quite deep shade, the ideal woody environment for orchids is one of dappled shade. If you are planting trees that you intend to grow orchids beneath, you'll need keep them well separated, so that both light and rain can get to the ground without too much dripping from the trees on to the plants beneath.

Figure 8.2 Dwarf fruit trees, like this 'Egremont Russet' apple, are ideal for the small garden.

Figure 8.3 Full-sized fruit trees need a lot of space.

up to the tree trunk for the annual cut of the understorey. For trees on dwarfing and semi-dwarfing rootstocks, where the trees are generally lower and the canopy more open, careful pruning will give space to get around the base of the trees to cut the grass. If the trees are too close together, not only will it be difficult to mow between the trees but also the denser shade may discourage summer-flowering species.

The best time for planting trees is autumn, while the ground is still warm from the summer and wet from autumn rains. If you buy your trees potted rather than bare-rooted, you can put them in during the spring and summer months but you will need to keep them well watered to ensure their survival.

WOODLAND TREE SPECIES

As well as fruit trees, woodland trees can be used to provide shade for woodland orchids. However, while some orchids can tolerate growing under evergreens, it's best to avoid conifers, and rhododendron is also unsuited to growing anything underneath. But apart from these exceptions, given enough space, most of our native deciduous trees will offer just the right conditions for woodland orchids.

Figure 8.4 This woodland ride, used by horses during the autumn and winter, supported a good population of Early Purple and Common Spotted Orchids.

Creating a real woodland glade needs space for the full effect, and if you have a lot of space you could plant a group of full-sized woodland trees - though sycamore is not a good idea, as in autumn the leaf litter can smother anything growing underneath it. However, you can also create a pleasing glade with just a few small garden trees or large shrubs, such as hawthorn or hazel. Hawthorn will form a nice symmetrical tree, while hazel tends towards a multi-stemmed shrub, and as long as they are not planted too close together, these species will make a charming area for woodland underplanting. For smaller spaces, the idea is to bring the canopy closer to the ground so that shade is supplied around the tree or shrub, rather than right underneath it.

A more striking glade in a small area can be made by planting Japanese maples, of which there are very many named varieties of different sizes. As elegant garden trees giving dappled-to-deep shade, they are hard to beat.

PLANTING AND MAINTAINING YOUR ORCHARD OR GLADE

Once your trees are in place, it's time to think about the orchids and their accompanying woodland flowers. The choice of species is discussed in the following pages, and planting guidance is given in Chapter 4. Try to plant your orchids when the ground is damp, either in spring or autumn, as this will give them time to establish their roots, so if the trees dry out the ground they will still be able to gain access to sufficient water.

When planting orchids in shady areas near trees, it's worth taking your time deciding where best to put them. Although this may seem obvious, it is especially important under trees. It's difficult to move orchids from around trees without causing them considerable, if not fatal, damage. First, the tree roots will be shallow and wide. It is unusual for all but a few roots to extend below 2m deep, and 80-90 per cent of tree roots are in the top 60cm of soil. So when the orchids are established, their roots will be inextricably linked with the trees they are planted around. Second, some orchid species, most notably the Violet Helleborine, have roots that extend 1m into the ground. Quite apart from them being entangled with the tree roots, these are so deep that it wouldn't be worth trying to move established plants.

After you have set out the plants, the amount of maintenance needed should be quite small. Try to keep the grass short by cutting at the end of the growing season, as described in Chapter 7. You will probably find that the grass is easier to keep under control than in an open area, because of the shade from the trees. If you are growing Helleborines, some of which enjoy the dappled shade under trees, it's best to put off the cutting time until very late, as they retain their green leaves right up until the seasonal frosts finally catch them. You could even cut in the spring, though at that point the grass and other old foliage will have started to rot and may be difficult to both cut and handle.

> *After you have set out the plants, the amount of maintenance needed should be quite small.*

CHOOSING YOUR ORCHIDS

Orchids and other types of woodland plant have adapted strategies to cope with the shade. There are two types of native woodland orchids: shade avoiders and shade tolerators. The Early Purple Orchid and Greater Butterfly Orchid are shade avoiders. Much of their growth is in spring and early summer, before the leaf canopy reaches its full extent. They also tend to grow in rides, clearings and wood margins, where the shade is not so intense. In the days when woodland was coppiced, these orchids would put on a good display in the years when the coppice had just been cut, and then grow without flowering in the following years.

Shade tolerators happily grow in shade and tend to flower later in the year, when the tree canopy is fully expanded. Their anatomy and physiology are adapted to produce food from photosynthesis at low light levels, so they tend to be slower-growing and can be damaged by high levels of light. Shade-tolerant orchids also have the advantage of being able to top up their food reserves from their fungal associate (a few have even gone to the extreme of losing their chlorophyll and living entirely off their fungal associate). Many of the Helleborines are shade tolerators.

Some orchid species that normally occur in open grassland can also grow under trees, where they will grow taller and more lanky, and be very susceptible to any competition from other plants growing with them.

Although the light level will be the main factor to consider when choosing orchids for an orchard or glade, it's also worth taking into account your soil type, so that the orchids are suited to the conditions into which your trees will be established. The following native orchid species are ideally suited to growing under trees. More details of these species can be found in Chapter 3.

Figure 8.5 An Early Purple Orchid growing with cowslips on a north-facing slope.

Early Purple Orchid

This cheerful orchid can be seen flowering from April onwards, before the tree canopy fully forms. It likes neutral or, better still, calcareous soils, but will tolerate a wide range. In woodland it often grows and flowers with bluebells, and can portray a beautiful touch of spring on a sunny hedge-bank (Fig. 8.5) with bluebells, primroses and greater stitchwort.

Greater Butterfly Orchid

Predominantly found in woods on calcareous soil, the charming Greater Butterfly Orchid can also grow on open hillsides in full sun. Under trees, the plants can be anything up to 60cm tall in good conditions. This is another shade-avoiding woodland species, mainly found in woodland clearings and margins. Its delicate white flower is unmistakable (Figs 8.6 and 8.7).

Figure 8.6 The Greater Butterfly Orchid in bud.

Figure 8.7 The Greater Butterfly Orchid in full flower.

Broad-leaved Helleborine

The traditionally accepted growing place for the Broad-leaved Helleborine is in beech woods on limestone, but in general they seem to grow well under most trees, except conifers. The stems can be nearly a metre high, depending on conditions. This is a very good example of a shade-tolerant species, being quite happy in continuous shade. It flowers relatively late in summer (Figs 8.8 and 8.9), and often 'pauses' below ground for a year or two after flowering.

Figures 8.8 and 8.9 Broad-leaved Helleborines can have quite a range of flower colours.

> *Choosing flowers to accompany orchids beneath trees can be tricky, as they should be shade-tolerant but not so prolific that they overpower the orchids.*

WOODLAND PLANTS TO INCLUDE WITH YOUR ORCHIDS

Choosing flowers to accompany orchids beneath trees can be tricky, as they should be shade-tolerant but not so prolific that they overpower the orchids. Although it may be tempting to opt for shade-loving ornamentals from the garden centre, that will produce an unbalanced collection of plants that look slightly dysfunctional. But with a little imagination, and with an eye to the species that would be found in the finest woodland glade, you can create a delightful patch. There are many spring flowers that produce lovely displays in woodland before the tree leaves unfurl, while light gets through to the forest floor.

With this in mind, we would recommend growing wild flowers under trees. Most woodland flowers are perennials or biennials. As they'll take longer than annuals to achieve flowering size, you might prefer to put plants in rather than sow seed.

While a garden flower bed might have an abundance of different flower types, in a semi-wild setting this isn't necessary for maximum effect. A flower bed has a collection of specimen plants, but your garden glade will have a few specimen plants - your orchids - with the spaces filled in with background growth that can be left to make the area look natural and established. Sometimes these wild flowers will turn up unexpectedly.

The following is a range of ground-cover plants that are quite at home under trees and will set off your woodland orchids beautifully. Recommended suppliers of these plants are listed in Resources.

Common Twayblade

Twayblades are not common any longer, though they are widespread. They are easy shade-tolerant growers once established, being happy in pastures and meadows as well as in shady woodland. Established plants can form whole colonies by means of the spreading rhizome. They give their display of green flower spikes in summer.

Violet Helleborine and Green-flowered Helleborine

In the wild, these species occur mostly in beech woods. The Violet Helleborine prefers chalky soils but seems to thrive in much deeper shade than the Broad-leaved Helleborine, so if you have a particularly shady area under trees on suitable soil, this would be perfect. The rare Green-flowered Helleborine has less shade tolerance but a wider soil tolerance, so is worth a try.

Figure 8.10 Dog's mercury with Early Purple Orchid.

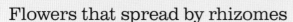

Figure 8.11 Dog's mercury with Butterfly Orchid.

Flowers that spread by rhizomes

Once established, plants with rhizomes can spread quite quickly, as the underground root system sends up new plant shoots as it grows. This can result in beautiful drifts of flowers: examples often seen in the countryside being wood anemone and lesser celandine. This type of plant is also easy to distribute, as replanted sections of the rhizome will quickly form another patch of flowers.

Dog's mercury

If you have an area with dense shade, then dog's mercury will grow well. It has a creeping rhizome, but it isn't invasive. It's always a pleasure to see this plant in woodlands, as it will often be found with Early Purple Orchids and Butterfly Orchids (Figs 8.10 and 8.11). The flowers of dog's mercury itself are very small and not particularly obvious (Fig. 8.12), and the plant is poisonous if eaten.

Lesser celandine

This plant grows well in shade but is quite happy in some sunshine. The flowers are vibrant yellow, on a spreading carpet of small, glossy green leaves (Fig. 8.13).

Wood anemone

The wood anemone has lovely white flowers which, though small, form drifts that can be spotted from some distance away. Indeed, wood anemones will form almost circular mats, as they grow evenly in all directions.

Wood sorrel

Wood sorrel also covers the ground effectively, with its charming trifoliate leaves borne on short petioles (leaf stalks). It thrives in shade and forms drifts of leaves and small, delicate white flowers.

Figure 8.12 The small flowers of dog's mercury. Despite its insignificant appearance, the plant is poisonous if eaten.

Flowers that spread by seed

Many woodland flowers spread by seed. It can take some time for them to come up to flowering size from seed, so putting in plants will give your display a head start. Once they are established, it shouldn't be necessary to replant, as they will be seeding themselves.

Bluebell

No flower could be more emblematic of a British woodland in springtime than the bluebell, brightening the dull colour of the ground with a

Figure 8.13 Lesser celandine is a pretty, spring-flowering ground-cover plant.

wash of sky blue (Fig. 8.14). If you want to grow bluebells, make sure you plant the native English species rather than the Spanish bluebell, which has a denser flower spike of a lighter blue and hybridizes with our native bluebell.

Foxglove

Amid the trees, every garden should have some foxgloves (Fig. 8.15). These lovely biennial flowers are the very epitome of shady lanes and woods. They produce seed in abundance, and once established the population will look after itself, the plants growing where they like. You don't need many foxgloves to give your garden a lovely country feel.

Lily of the valley

Along with any bluebells you may be growing, it's interesting to add in another spreading upright flower like lily of the valley. Its delicate spikes of white flowers are not dissimilar to the

Figure 8.14 A carpet of bluebells in springtime is the jewel in the crown of any woodland glade.

Figure 8.15 Foxgloves are a perfect woodland complement to any garden.

bluebell in shape, and it has a delightful scent. It is very happy in shade.

Lords-and-ladies

Also known as cuckoo pint, lords-and-ladies is often seen in hedgerows and shady woodland, both as single plants and small clumps. The flower is one of the most easily recognized in the countryside, as its structure is confined to two species in the UK, this one and Italian lords-and-ladies. Both these flowers have a cowl, called a spathe, which partially covers the central spadix, or spike of minute flowers. The decorative show carries on in the autumn, when the central flower column remains standing with bright orange berries containing the seeds. The berries are poisonous.

Primrose

Primroses are a good example of the beautiful and subtle nature of wild flowers. They are exquisite in the early part of the year as archetypal spring flowers. Most people see them during daylight, but when you grow them in your own garden you'll notice the almost glowing colour they radiate at twilight, a reminder that the garden doesn't stop being lovely just because the light has fled.

Ramsons

Some species are rather good at seeding themselves locally and forming quite large colonies in the right conditions. One of these is ramsons, or wild garlic (Fig. 8.16). This is a species that likes damp and shady conditions, so if you have a shady area that doesn't dry out, this is the plant for you. As ramsons is a type of garlic, you can use the leaves in salads and the bulbs to cook with. The flowers are very much like a white onion flower and also edible. If the plant becomes invasive, it is easily controlled by eating the bulbs.

Early Purple Orchid (*Orchis mascula*).

Figure 8.16 Ramsons in flower. The leaves and flowers are delicious in salads, and the bulbs can be used as garlic.

Snowdrop

In among the bluebells there's always room for some snowdrops. These grow very well in turf under trees as well as between other flowers, but they are easily pushed out, so some care is needed over time to make sure they survive.

IN SUMMARY

A woodland habitat in your garden offers the opportunity to grow a range of orchids that appreciate some shade, such as the Greater Butterfly, the Early Purple, the Common Twayblade and the Broad-leaved and Violet Helleborines. These will look beautiful against a background of carefully chosen wild flowers.

By creating a shady area, you will be providing a very important environment, one that is often underrated in gardens. A glade of even just a few trees is a valuable ecosystem. Trees provide structure and cover not only for the shade-loving plants beneath but also for wildlife: birds will arrive, and you may see bats and other woodland species such as the speckled wood butterfly. If you plant an orchard, you will have not only a charming space to enjoy but also food for yourself and the wildlife.

Chapter Nine

ORCHIDS
in rockeries or damp ground

The majority of British native orchids prefer alkaline soil conditions. If you live in an area with a chalky soil - as in much of the
south of England, East Anglia, the Humber and parts of Yorkshire
- then you will be able to grow many native orchid species in your
garden. If you have a more clay-based or heavy acid soil, however,
the options for growing chalk-hill orchids are more limited. You can
grow them in containers, or, as we described in Chapter 4, replace
the immediate area of soil when planting out your orchids. Or you
can dig out a whole flower bed and replace the soil with a high-lime
mix. The drawback of the latter two options is that the soil will very
slowly revert to acid with drainage and slow mixing by invertebrates
such as worms.

A better way to solve the problem is to build a rockery.

Opposite: Bee Orchid (*Ophrys apifera*) with quaking-grass (*Briza media*), mouse-ear hawkweed
(*Pilosella officinarum*) and wild thyme (*Thymus polytrichus*). Limestone grassland in mid-June.

Fig 9.1 Many of our native orchid species prefer calcareous soil, as found on a limestone hillside such as this.

Rockeries aren't particularly fashionable at the present time, but they allow plants to be independent of the surrounding soil type and also to be shown off to their very best advantage. This chapter explains how to set up a rockery and grow orchids in rockeries with companion plants.

If you are lucky enough to have a patch in your garden that is permanently damp or, better still, wet, you can grow some of our very special orchid species. (Some devotees even build a bog garden specifically for the purpose.) Such a project is beyond the scope of this chapter, but on pages 154-155 we discuss growing native orchids that thrive in or have a tolerance for wet conditions.

CREATING AN ORCHID ROCKERY

Before you start building a rockery, bear in mind that, in contrast to a garden meadow, a rockery is a more-or-less permanent feature. So think carefully about where you site it, and how much space to use. Don't plan your rockery near trees, as most orchids need sun; also, when autumn comes, falling leaves will accumulate in the nooks and crannies. It can be almost impossible to clear a rockery of fallen leaves and they not only make it look untidy but also smother many of the plants.

Once you have chosen the site, there are several points to consider:

- Decide if you want a flat bed or a sloping one. Both types give you a contained space in which you can define the soil type.
- Remove the soil before you start building.
- If you have a loamy topsoil, mix enough garden lime into it to change the character of it completely before putting it back into the rockery.
- If you have a clay soil, or one with a very high organic content, replace this with a loam-based compost that has been mixed with lime (see 'Your orchid species', page 152)

Flat-bed rockeries

Despite the term 'flat bed', this type of rockery still needs to be raised at least slightly above the level of the surrounding garden, so that the soil type in the rockery can be different from the base material. If the rockery is raised well above the ground, it will be a raised bed with a distinct structure to it (Fig. 9.3). This sort of raised rockery is most often seen with alpine plants in it, which is a good way of showing off your orchids, as the alpine plants will be quite short. If you are going to have a retaining wall around your raised bed, work out on graph paper what shape and height you want for your rockery. This will help you calculate the amount of walling material needed and the volume of soil or compost required to fill it.

Figure 9.2 A flat-bed rockery at ground level allows the whole area to be viewed with ease. This can be planted with rockery plants and orchids, which complement each other.

Figure 9.3 A flat-bed rockery raised above the ground, which makes it both easier to work on and to appreciate smaller rockery plants.

Another option is to create a low mound shape, where instead of a retaining wall at the edge, the shape is formed by piling large rocks together in the middle, with soil between them (Fig 9.2). (See below for considerations when choosing rock.)

If building a retaining wall, then timber (in the form of railway sleepers), brick or stone are the best materials to use if you want the structure to last. Brick or stone are the most durable as well as the most expensive and time-consuming to construct. If the stone is limestone, it will encourage soil alkalinity. Both brick and stone need to be mortared in with a weatherproof mortar so that the structure doesn't disintegrate in frost.

An alternative is a drystone wall, which is the most aesthetic choice, as it blends naturally into the environment. Drystone walls also allow for planting in the nooks and crannies, and have very good drainage, but they can be difficult to stabilize without practice. So if you intend on building a drystone wall yourself, consider going on a training course so you can complete the job with your own hands.

Sloping rockeries

Sloping rockeries can be constructed in one of two different styles or, if you have space, in a mixture of both. These are: as an outcrop, where the rocks are at different levels down the slope; and as a terrace, where the rocks form a series of terraced steps. If the rocks are too small or badly positioned, it will look odd and rather artificial.

The choice of rock is an entirely personal one, but quarried rock is the most pleasing to look at and will weather the best. Avoid broken concrete or reconstituted stone. Limestone is best of all, as it weathers wonderfully, provides nooks and crannies for mosses and liverworts, and is suitable for chalk-loving orchids. Do not remove stones from the countryside – this destroys natural habitats and can damage a natural ecosystem.

Dig into the slope so that each rock can be settled on a ledge with a large proportion of it covered with soil, to avoid disrupting the line of the slope. To create an outcrop effect, position the rocks deliberately randomly. If you prefer a terrace, position the rocks evenly.

Settle your chosen rocks on a bed of fine grit or sand. This will help bed the rocks in and stop them moving over time - or, worse still, the first time that you have a downpour or step on them. They should be steady enough to step on immediately, or they will shift at some point in the future. It is easier to make a permanent rockery with large stones, in many ways the bigger the better. There will always be some settling over time, but the movement will be less noticeable with larger rocks.

Your orchid species

If you plan to grow Bee Orchids, Pyramidal Orchids or Chalk Fragrant Orchids (Fig 9.4), then add 25-50 per cent garden lime to your soil or compost. If you use a commercial compost, it should be loam-based, such as John Innes No. 2 (see Chapter 4, page 77), not peat-based or multipurpose compost, which has a

Figure 9.5 The versatile Common Spotted Orchid.

high organic content. A mixture of about 30 per cent lime to 70 per cent loam will also suit other more easy-going species such as the Common Spotted Orchid (Fig 9.5).

Once you have a loam-and-lime mix in the above proportions, you shouldn't need to check the pH, as you know it will be a high-calcium, alkaline mixture.

Rockeries are ideal for calcium-loving orchids that thrive best in full sun and in soil that drains freely (Fig. 9.6), but not so ideal for other species. See Chapter 3 for details of the preferred soil conditions of each of the orchid species we recommend for cultivation.

Plants to go with your orchids

Companion planting with orchids on a sunny calcareous rockery can be very decorative, with either native wild flowers or domestic varieties of chalk-hill plants and alpine species. When

Figure 9.4 The Chalk Fragrant Orchid is a typical species of calcareous grassland.

Figure 9.6 The Bee Orchid is another classic chalk-hill species, thriving in sun and a free-draining alkaline soil.

planting up your rockery, keep any companion plants with a strong spreading habit well away from the orchids to ensure they don't overgrow them.

Rockery companion plants in poor soil won't be very fast growers so will need little control on a seasonal basis. Restricting your companion planting to alpine species will keep the overall height of the plants low, against which the orchids will stand out clearly. Most alpine plants are fairly slow growers and perennial, so they won't need replanting every year.

The following are companion plants that are worth considering:

- **Alpine yarrow** grows to about 15cm high and doesn't spread much more than that sideways.
- **Blue-eyed grass** is a small alpine perennial that is also quite happy seeding itself.
- **Bugle** is another native perennial that is quite

comfortable in a rockery, but it does spread by runners so needs to be controlled.

- Many ***Campanula*** species fit well with an alpine theme, but in the same genus there are some large and inappropriate species. The bellflowers in this genus are all delicate blue native plants.
- ***Dianthus*** species, which range in size from carnations that are normally associated with wedding buttonholes to small alpine pinks. Some of these, such as Deptford pink and maiden pink, are native wild flowers.
- **Houseleeks** are varied and spread slowly. These are native to the Mediterranean.
- **Mount Atlas daisy** is an alpine flower that only reaches 5cm high but it forms lovely cushions of flowers.
- **Saxifrages** come in a huge range of colours and types. They all spread widely, but grow slowly and need little annual attention. Some are native species, but many of the most decorative are alpines.
- ***Sedum*** is another genus of plants with a wide range of colours and sizes. Although they spread quite easily, they are slow and not really invasive. Our native species are called stonecrops.
- **Snow-in-summer** and **aubretia**. No discussion of a rock garden is complete without mentioning these two favourites. They are both prolific producers of late spring flowers and vigorous spreaders, so will need annual control.

Once you have set up a rockery for your chosen orchids, the aim is to grow them with a range of alpine and native chalk-hill plants that will emphasize their charms and delight. Choose accompanying plants that don't need a great deal of attention, both to avoid making extra work for yourself but also, more importantly, so as not to disturb the soil in the rockery. While any offspring from the alpines or wild flowers will be visible within a year, any seeds dropped by your orchids will take several years before they show signs of producing a leaf. The plants will be most vulnerable during these early years, because as you dig or weed your rockery you won't know whether you are disturbing them. When the plants have recognizable leaves above ground, you can be very pleased with yourself for having produced a microhabitat that has encouraged and supported a developing population of native orchids.

ORCHIDS IN DAMP GROUND

The choice of orchids for damp ground depends on the amount and nature of the water present. Plants in areas subject to winter flooding shouldn't be a problem, as most orchids are dormant in winter. However, cold, wet standing water can cause problems when the plants start growing in the spring. So standing water requires a different approach, with marsh species being the best suited to this situation (Fig. 9.7).

Dactylorhiza Marsh Orchids

All of our native marsh orchids are found in the genus *Dactylorhiza*, and four species are suitable for the garden: the Northern Marsh, Southern Marsh, Early Marsh and Narrow-leaved Marsh. This particular genus produces hybrids between species with ease, depending on how close they are growing to each other, as pollinating insects flit at random between flowers. This makes it difficult to maintain colonies of individual species, but the resulting hybrids can be very large and lovely in their own right. Marsh orchids, like all the

Figure 9.7 Marsh Helleborines are very pretty plants for a wet area, and can produce dense clumps of flowers.

Dactylorhiza species, are quite easy-going about the conditions in which they thrive, but the main thing they do not like is deep shade. The soil substrate doesn't seem to affect them unduly – they will happily grow on both peat bogs and on flooded limestone quarry workings.

Marsh Helleborine

In contrast to *Dactylorhiza* marsh orchids, which tend to grow as individuals or in small clumps, the Marsh Helleborine can form quite dense clumps from creeping rhizomes (Fig. 9.7). Marsh Helleborines do best on neutral-to-alkaline soils. They seem to do very well in limestone areas, which is worth bearing in mind if you are constructing a damp or boggy area from scratch.

Damp-tolerant species

While the above orchid species are adapted to living with their roots in damp conditions, some of our other native species can nevertheless tolerate wet ground. We have seen the Common Spotted Orchid growing on the edge of a pond, flowering to all intents and purposes in water.

Sometimes, if the ground is alkaline and wet but very free-draining, it is possible to grow Chalk Fragrant Orchids.

Plants to go with orchids in a boggy area

You will want companion plants that will not overpower your orchids. Grasses will be quickly invasive, as they form mats of roots that smother any other plant while they themselves do not become waterlogged. Be very careful in your choices, as some species, such as the ornamental rhubarbs (*Rheum* species) and *Gunnera* species, can become very large. Water mint is another bog plant that can be grown, but it is as invasive as any mint. The following are some good options to try.

- **Butterworts** are carnivorous plants with very pale leaves and pretty flowers. There are some lovely native species among them, though the non-natives are slightly bigger and more colourful.
- **Cardinal flower** is a tall lobelia from North America, growing up to a metre high.
- **Ferns** (but not bracken) form a pretty backdrop in damp places, and there are many native species that will settle in easily.
- **Hostas**, while not native, are very decorative.
- *Ranunculus* species, specifically native water buttercups and spearworts. These are often grown in water, but as long as they are in damp and boggy conditions, they are happy.

- *Sarracenia* species are pitcher plants from America, some of which are hardy in Britain, such as *S. purpurea*. This species stands about 15cm tall and looks every inch the carnivorous plant.
- **Sundews** are generally grown for their leaves, which are covered in tendrils with sticky tips that they use to trap small insects, but they also have interesting flowers. Again, these plants include some attractive natives. Like the butterworts, sundews are easily overwhelmed by vigorous plants, so it's best not to grow them with buttercups or mints.

IN SUMMARY

Setting up a specialist area for your orchids, whether a rockery or a bog garden, will not only extend the range of species you can grow but also create focal points of interest in your garden. The two specialist ecosystems described here will support a range of companion plants that are a delight in themselves, from small alpine flowers to fly-catching sundews. The wider range of plant species will also increase biodiversity by encouraging a greater range of insect life.

The artificial construction of a habitat in a garden does take a certain amount of work, but it is well worth the effort. With a bog garden you also have the option of introducing some of our native carnivorous plants, which require a very poor soil and generally do very well with orchid companions.

Chapter Ten

Repopulating
WILD AREAS

There is something very exciting about restoring a derelict site, whether it is an old meadow, a hillside, an orchard or woodland, changing it from an area of limited plant range to a haven of biodiversity. Establishing orchids need not be a reintroduction: it can be a new addition to the ecosystem. Although orchids have specific requirements regarding their symbiotic fungal associate, just because the orchids are not there does not mean the fungus isn't. And if a suitable fungal symbiont is present in the soil, you can establish orchid plants that will reproduce and go on to form a stable colony.

Opposite: Marsh Helleborine (*Epipactis palustris*) with ragged robin (*Lychnis flos-cuculi*), lesser spearwort (*Ranunculus flammula*) and fen bedstraw (*Galium uliginosum*). Marsh in late June.

Introducing native orchids into a suitable wild environment is a laudable thing to do, whether or not it has a known pedigree as an orchid site. Instead of a garden, you will be creating a self-sustaining area of highly diverse life, both botanical and zoological.

You will need patience, as it will take several years to create a balanced and prolific ecosystem, as seen in Fig. 10.1, but it will be worth it. A derelict meadow will be either vegetation going to scrub or improved pasture with nitrogen-rich soil ideal for grass growth. An old orchard will have a few remaining trees, probably not fruiting very well but still standing, with a lot of brambles and scrub present. The same is broadly true of neglected or badly managed woodland. Brambles seem to get established given any chance at all. If you are lucky, you will start with an area where some native flora is already in place; if you are not so lucky, you will have a piece of land that has been in agricultural use and that needs considerable restoration.

Whichever type of land you have, the basic practicalities to consider when introducing orchids into the flora are:

- What type of soil do you have?
- Has the ground been treated with fertilizer or weedkiller?
- How wet is the site? Are there marsh patches?
- How shady is the site? Does it face south, for instance?
- Are there any records of orchids growing there in the past?

CHANGES IN WILD ORCHID POPULATIONS

While books on wild flowers and guides to orchid natural history state that these plants have very specific requirements, it is not always so. They can be remarkably flexible if they are not unduly stressed by competition. When plants have such a convoluted life cycle as orchids do, it doesn't take much to disrupt it in the form of either chemical or mechanical interference. Chemical interference is by either weedkiller or fertilizer, while mechanical interference is the plough or inappropriate mowing times. Most herbicides have a limited life in the soil, but fertilizers are different and will have to be lived with until they have leached out of the soil.

Sites where these practices have not occurred are quite rare, and are generally on land described as marginal, i.e. areas with thin and poor topsoil of low fertility. With the gradual intensification of land use, such undisturbed

Figure 10.1 An established meadow with Early Purple Orchids and cowslips.

land has mostly become restricted to upland areas of chalk hills and moors, where we now see our most abundant collections of orchids. Old and ancient woodland also comes into this category and is therefore still a place to find orchids, though the number of species is smaller than that found in open environments.

For those who want to reclaim an area and enhance its biodiversity with native orchids, the good news is that most orchids have a very wide potential range. Descriptions found in specialist guides to orchids dating from the nineteenth century show how common and widespread these plants once were.

The list of areas with current orchid populations is shown on the website of the Botanical Society of Britain and Ireland (BSBI) - see Resources. These populations are nurtured, but areas barren of orchids remain so until and unless the plants are reintroduced.

> *Undisturbed land has mostly become restricted to upland chalk hills and moors, where we now see our most abundant collections of orchids.*

The associated fungi

One often forgotten thing about ecosystems is that they work in several dimensions. Below ground, roots and tunnelling extend several metres. Above ground, the fruiting bodies of fungi are the toadstools and mushrooms that sprout up from time to time. The fungi are normally underground and play an important part in the decomposition process.

Where the fungal associate found with an orchid species is always the same, then it is essential for the orchid's growth. Where the orchid is not so choosy in its fungus, the seeds can germinate and the plants prosper more widely. For most orchid species, the problem of seed germination is not always the presence of a fungal symbiont; rather, it's whether the fungus can make contact with the seed before it falls prey to an enemy, which might be anything from a slug to a bacterial infection.

There are situations where the fungal symbiont has disappeared from soil that has been heavily treated with fungicide, either deliberately or inadvertently, as runoff from crops. Excessive and repeated use of a chemical mix such as Bordeaux mixture, used extensively in the control of mildews in food crops, will upset the balance of fungi in the soil: in the case of Bordeaux mixture, continuous annual use results in copper in the soil, which kills earthworms as well. Most other available fungicides have a limited period of activity, so when you reintroduce your orchids you will also be safely reintroducing their symbiotic fungus, which will already be on their roots and in their potting compost.

CHOOSING SUITABLE ORCHID SPECIES

There are several ways to work out which species will suit your area. Start by taking a good look at the site. If you have a slope, the direction it faces will make a difference. A south-facing slope will be warmer and drier than any other. Shade is also important, as are any standing damp patches, or areas that are so free-draining they contain only deep-rooted perennials. Find out about the soil type and look at what species are growing there already. If you can, try to find out which orchids used to grow there. Doing all of this will prevent you putting plants in the wrong place, where they will not thrive.

Local history

Contact a local horticultural society and ask if anyone remembers seeing orchids in the area: you may be surprised what you hear. Look at old memoirs and local history books, if any exist. If you are in an area of intrinsic natural interest, there may be a book on the local natural history (Fig. 10.2), which will give you a good idea of the original flora and fauna.

If you are determined to find out which species used to grow in an area, visit your local museum to see if they have any local herbarium collections.

Assess or test the soil

Ideally, you would repopulate an area with the species that were there originally. But if you don't know this, you can find out what sort of orchids you would expect to find there by assessing the soil type. For example, does it contain a lot of organic material or a lot of limestone, or does it have a limestone rock base? All

Figure 10.2 This meadow was described in a book by Norman Hickin as having Early Purple, Common Spotted and Green-winged Orchids. It is now improved pasture, favouring vigorous grass growth at the expense of other species.

of these can affect the pH, taking it towards or away from chalk-hill species.

Sometimes it takes only a glance to ascertain that the soil is very alkaline, and so would have supported all the most commonly found chalk-loving species, such as Bee and Pyramidal Orchids. Otherwise use a soil-testing kit and/or dig a hole to see how deep the soil is and what the base rock is. If you go down beyond 25cm without reaching a rock layer, and the soil is of loam, it is most likely acidic.

Assess the existing wild flowers

Take a detailed look at what wild flowers are still surviving there. They may be tucked away in field corners or road verges, but they would have been more widespread in earlier times. If there is an obvious natural species community, you shouldn't need to test the soil in any detail. Given a good population of wild flowers, a reasonably good field guide to identify them will tell you what sort of soil and terrain they like to grow in. Then you can match your orchid species to the same soil type.

PLANTING YOUR SITE

There are broadly three types of environment that can be repopulated with orchids: grassland, woodland and quarry. Treat each of these in the same way that you would an original colonization of, say, a meadow, an orchard or a massive rockery - as described in Chapters 7, 8 and 9. If the site has wet or boggy areas within it, these will take slightly different species.

The difference between repopulation projects and domestic-scale growing is the need for extra patience and money. With large projects, obviously, it is necessary to introduce far more plants than would be required in a garden. What might be manageable in a garden is best broken down into smaller areas for a larger project. Since the aim is to introduce a sustainable population, the more plants you put in, the better. For a field or woodland of any size, start with an area where you can put in plants at the rate of one per square metre. For a more striking effect, plant the orchids closer together than this, but to ensure pollination it is best not to space them any further apart. They should be there for many years, seeding and spreading locally. If you decide to speed up the population spread before the seeds have produced plants, plant up a wider area.

If you have the patience to wait several years before you get orchids ready for planting out, then you could try raising your own plants from seed, as described in Chapter 5; this is a good way of producing plants in quantity. If you would prefer to plant orchids that are already growing and able to survive outside, see Chapter 4 for advice on sourcing these.

Before planting anything, though, look at the site in its entirety, as described earlier. Once you have assessed it in terms of sun, shade, drainage, dampness and any variation in soil

> *The difference between repopulation projects and domestic-scale growing is the need for extra patience and money.*

type, draw a map showing this detail. This way you can keep track of where you have planted your orchids and look forward to a repopulation that will be carried out only once.

Planting your orchids in a wild area is done in the same way as described in Chapter 4. As they are native plants - fully hardy and, once rooted, robust - they shouldn't need any particular further attention. There may be some losses from molluscs or other predation, but in a wild environment these will be surprisingly light.

Introducing other wild flowers

The wild plants you would find associated with your orchids in their natural habitats can be introduced by distributing seed by hand. See Chapters 7-9 for suggestions for native species. Many of these - grassland flowers such as hawkbits, knapweeds, ox-eye daisies (Fig. 10.3) and plantains - are perennials, so will need to be seeded only once, after which they will look after themselves if you look after the environment (see below). Annuals are also a key component of a natural ecosystem, and in an open area yellow rattle is probably the most useful, as it helps to control the grass. If you visit an already established meadow or woodland, you will notice that stands of single species are very rare. So when you scatter seed, keep the species composition as mixed as possible.

An alternative way of introducing perennials is to buy small plants, available as plugs. While this gives a quick result, it can be very expensive for repopulating a large area, so seed is the best option, though it will take two years before any flowers appear. The other advantage of seed is that those that germinate and survive will have found the best place for them, helping to give the replanted area a much more natural feel.

For some species, such as foxgloves in woodland, the ease with which seed can be obtained, either by bulk purchase or from a plant in your garden, makes it ideal for scattering among the trees. But beware the cultivated varieties as some, particularly foxgloves, look out of place in a natural habitat, whereas the natural grace and elegance of wild-type foxgloves cannot be

improved on. The suppliers listed in Resources are those that specialize in wild-type species and can offer seed in quite large quantities, which helps keep costs down.

ONGOING CARE

As with all wildlife restoration projects, the target of building a stable ecosystem with as wide a range of species as possible is a long-term one. If you look after the orchids with some basic management, you'll be surprised at what else will arrive with no intervention on your part. In the case of meadows, such management will involve an annual cut and/or winter grazing. With quarries and woodlands, you'll need to keep the understorey open at ground level to control encroaching scrub. It goes without saying: avoid using fertilizer or weedkiller.

By making an environment ideally suited to your orchids, you will have created an ideal environment for all the other plants and animals that naturally occur alongside them.

GENETIC DIVERSITY IN COLONY FORMATION

It doesn't do to be too narrow in one's view about the composition and identity of an orchid population, as the original way to prevent inbreeding no longer exists.

Due to agricultural changes over the last century, orchid populations have shrunk and in some cases disappeared. The remaining populations are not inherently unique - they form a collection of relict populations which, without both an increase in number and cross-fertilization with other populations, constitute a very fragile example of reduced genetic diversity.

This fragmentation of orchid populations means that what were once overlapping ranges

Figure 10.3 Ox-eye daisies.

Figure 10.4 A self-sustaining colony of Early Purple Orchids in a woodland setting.

For large areas, the more plants you can get in from as wide an origin as possible, the better. If you are going to put in Marsh and Spotted Orchids, you can reasonably expect them to form hybrids as they are notoriously promiscuous.

are now geographically isolated. This overlapping of range was important in keeping the level of inbreeding to a relatively low level, by the exchange of pollen and seed between areas; but now it is commonplace to have an isolated population only capable of pollinating itself. While bumblebees will happily forage more than 400m from home, and honeybees can range over 10km, this isn't far compared with the distance between two orchid populations; and even though bees may range that far, it doesn't mean they will be visiting the orchids. Weaker flying insects will have a shorter foraging range, restricting the potential for cross-fertilization between different populations even further.

To reduce the risk of inbreeding, obtain plants and seeds from as many different sources as possible. If you decide to grow your own plants, try to find a friendly landowner who has orchids you might take seeds from, or buy seed from a variety of origins. Alternatively, buy a few plants from different suppliers, then save seed from them. It is also best to introduce several plants at a time; that way you have a much better chance of setting up a self-sustaining population (Fig. 10.4).

IN SUMMARY

Repopulating an area of countryside with native orchids is perhaps the pinnacle of achievement for the native-orchid grower. It is one of the kindest things you can do to the land, however small the plot, because in order to create a sustainable orchid population, you will be bringing an entire ecosystem back to life.

Such a project should be undertaken slowly and with consideration for what is growing and what can grow in the conditions, so it is important to assess your site carefully. Wild areas are intrinsically unruly and very much slower to develop than gardens. Find out if there has been any fertilizer, herbicide or fungicide used, as this will help in understanding the plants.

Introduce orchid species that will be at home and will therefore help to establish a stable ecosystem. Work with the land: if plants won't grow, they are probably unsuited to the soil. Pay attention, do some research, and try to identify species that have been there before, as it is these that are likely to thrive. In this way you will produce a beautiful environment for all to enjoy - including all the wildlife that will arrive in its own time, demonstrating by its very presence the vigour and diversity of life.

Case study: repopulating a hillside meadow

This hillside of gently sloping grass in north Worcestershire is about 1.5 hectares in size – not large, but big enough for horses to have been kept on it (Fig. 10.5). The centre section is a raised and, in some places, exposed sandstone outcrop with very thin soil. However, the area was not conducive to grazing and so hadn't had horses on it for some time. Over the years it became colonized by plants, which the horses would have eaten or trampled.

The first task was a walk-around survey of the plants that were present. This needed to be done in spring and summer, so we could get an idea of the dominant species. The area was easily divided into four basic zones, even though the soil was the same throughout the field: free-draining, sandy and slightly acidic, with very low nutrients; it dried out and warmed in the sun very quickly. The four main areas were:

- The bottom of the field, which was the most nitrogen-rich as this is where the horses used to urinate.
- The centre section, dominated by scrub and a single ash tree.
- The south-facing slope, which had a lot of bracken on it.
- The top of the field, which was very dry.

Looking at the existing plants showed that the soil hadn't been fertilized or treated with weedkiller for a long time. There were

Figure 10.5 A hillside meadow of scrub and grass.

cowslips, knapweed and white campion in among the grasses, of which there were a number of different species. The scrub was mainly gorse and hawthorn, with brambles and some privet (Fig. 10.6).

Clearing the site

Removing some of the smaller gorse bushes and all of the privet allowed us to control the encroaching scrub. It was important to remove the privet, as this is a non-native of very little ecological value. Controlling brambles was also a mechanical activity and needs to be carried out annually, but getting rid of them entirely isn't necessary in an area of this scale.

More difficult to control were bracken and nettles. Bracken is notorious and takes patience to get under control by trampling and rolling – a simple but time-consuming process, so this is a continuing summer activity. Nettles prefer nitrogen-rich areas and are tenacious if left to grow unfettered. Here,

Figure 10.6 The predominant scrub species was invasive gorse.

Figure 10.7 Primroses make an early show in the meadow after introduction to the shady parts of the scrub.

cutting and constant disturbance has reduced the numbers a lot.

Introducing new plant species

New species were introduced in appropriate places. The first were primroses, positioned around the edges of the scrub (Fig. 10.7). These were put in as plants so that their progress could be monitored while the rest of the site was being returned to meadow grass and associated wild flowers. They took very well and seeded themselves.

Yellow rattle, poppy and oxeye daisy were introduced as seed. The original knapweed and white campion were left undisturbed until they had finished flowering, then the area was cut. The presence of some ragwort made the grass unsuitable as hay, so a stack was made – in which various species of wildlife, such as woodlice and slow-worms, took up residence.

The introduction of orchid species started with Common Spotted Orchids, which have taken well, at both the bottom and top of the field. Green-winged Orchids were then introduced in areas that have naturally short grass, halfway up the slope. As the soil is very sandy with very little organic matter in it, we thought Pyramidal Orchids would establish. These have naturalized well at the very top of the slope above the scrub, where it dries out in the summer. The long roots ensure the orchids can bring up moisture and nutrients from deep in the ground. In the future, Bee Orchids will be added to the list, as will Early Purple Orchids in the shadier areas around the scrub edges, alongside the primroses.

The development of this plot continues. Returning, or developing, a meadow for naturalizing orchids doesn't give instant results but takes time. Indeed, a year might pass before you know if a plant has taken and become a permanent resident.

PLANT LIST 1: COMMON TO LATIN NAMES

Alpine yarrow = *Achillea tomentosa*
Annual beard grass = *Polypogon monspeliensis*
Annual meadow grass = *Poa annua*
Apple = *Malus domestica*
Apple 'Egremont Russet' = *Malus domestica* 'Egremont Russet'
Aubrietas = *Aubrieta spp.*
Autumn Lady's Tresses = *Spiranthes spiralis*
Basil = *Ocimum basilicum*
Bee Orchid = *Ophrys apifera*
Bellflowers = *Campanula spp.*
Bird's-nest Orchid = *Neottia nidus-avis*
Black medick = *Medicago lupulina*
Blackberry = *Rubus fruticosus agg.*
Blue cupidone = *Catananche caerulea*
Blue daisy = *Catananche caerulea*
Blue flax = *Linum perenne*
Blue-eyed grass = *Sisyrinchium bellum*
Bluebell = *Hyacinthoides non-scripta*
Bog Orchid = *Hammarbya paludosa*
Bracken = *Pteridium aquilinum*
Bramble = *Rubus fruticosus agg.*
Breadfruit = *Artocarpus altilis*
Broad-leaved dock = *Rumex obtusifolius*
Broad-leaved Helleborine = *Epipactis helleborine*
Bugle = *Ajuga reptans*
Burnt Orchid = *Orchis ustulata*
Butterworts = *Pinguicula spp.*
Cardinal flower = *Lobelia cardinalis*
Cattleya = *Cattleya labiata*
Chalk Fragrant Orchid = *Gymnadenia conopsea*
Common cottongrass = *Eriophorum angustifolium*
Common Fragrant Orchid = *Gymnadenia conopsea*
Common knapweed = *Centaurea nigra*
Common poppy = *Papaver rhoeas*
Common restharrow = *Ononis repens*
Common rockrose = *Helianthemum nummularium*
Common Spotted Orchid = *Dactylorhiza fuchsii*
Common Twayblade = *Neottia ovata*
Coralroot Orchid = *Corallorhiza trifida*
Coriander = *Coriandrum sativum*
Cornflower = *Centaurea cyanus*
Cowslip = *Primula veris*
Creeping Jenny = *Lysimachia nummularia*
Creeping Lady's Tresses = *Goodyera repens*
Creeping willow = *Salix repens*
Crested dog's tail = *Cynosurus cristatus*
Cuckoo pint = *Arum maculatum*
Cuckooflower = *Cardamine pratensis*
Curled Odontoglossum = *Odontoglossum crispum*
Curled plantain lily = *Hosta crispula*

Dandelion = *Taraxacum officinale agg.*
Dark-red Helleborine = *Epipactis atrorubens*
Dense-flowered Orchid = *Neotinea maculata*
Deptford pink = *Dianthus armeria*
Devil's bit scabious = *Succisa pratensis*
Dewberry = *Rubus caesius*
Dog's mercury = *Mercurialis perennis*
Dune Helleborine = *Epipactis dunensis*
Dutchman's breeches = *Dicentra cucullaria*
Dwarf Purple Orchid = *Dactylorhiza purpurella*
Early Marsh Orchid = *Dactylorhiza incarnata*
Early Purple Orchid = *Orchis mascula*
Early Spider Orchid = *Ophrys sphegodes*
European Pear = *Pyrus communis*
Evergreen maidenhair = *Adiantum venustum*
Eyebright = *Euphrasia officinalis agg.*
Fen bedstraw = *Galium uliginosum*
Fen Orchid = *Liparis loeselii*
Field scabious = *Knautia arvensis*
Fly Orchid = *Ophrys insectifera*
Foxglove = *Digitalis purpurea*
Frog Orchid = *Coeloglossum viride*
Garden Privet = *Ligustrum ovalifolium*
Ghost Orchid = *Epipogium aphyllum*
Giant rhubarbs = *Gunnera spp.*
Glaucous sedge = *Carex flacca*
Gorse = *Ulex europaeus*
Greater Butterfly Orchid = *Platanthera chlorantha*
Greater knapweed = *Centaurea scabiosa*
Greater plantain = *Plantago major*
Greater stitchwort = *Stellaria holostea*
Greater Tongue Orchid = *Serapias lingua*
Green-flowered Helleborine = *Epipactis phyllanthes*
Green-veined Orchid = *Anacamptis morio*
Green-winged Orchid = *Anacamptis morio*
Hare's tail grass = *Lagurus ovatus*
Hawkbits = *Leontodon spp.*
Hawkweed = *Pilosella*
Hawthorn = *Crataegus monogyna*
Hazel = *Corylus avellana*
Heath Fragrant Orchid = *Gymnadenia borealis*
Heath Spotted Orchid = *Dactylorhiza maculata*
Hebridean Marsh Orchid = *Dactylorhiza ebudensis*
Herb robert = *Geranium robertianum*
Himalayan maidenhair = *Adiantum venustum*
Horse chestnut = *Aesculus hippocastanum*
Hostas = *Hosta spp.*
Houseleeks = *Sempervivum spp.*
Irish Lady's Tresses = *Spiranthes romanzoffiana*
Irish Marsh Orchid = *Dactylorhiza occidentalis*
Italian lords-and-ladies = *Arum italicum*

How to grow NATIVE ORCHIDS in gardens large and small

Japanese maple = *Acer palmatum*
Kidney vetch = *Anthyllis vulneraria*
Lady Orchid = *Orchis purpurea*
Lady's Slipper Orchid = *Cypripedium calceolus*
Lady's smock = *Cardamine pratensis*
Lapland Marsh Orchid = *Dactylorhiza traunsteinerioides subsp. Lapponica*
Late Spider Orchid = *Ophrys fuciflora*
Lesser Butterfly Orchid = *Platanthera bifolia*
Lesser celandine = *Ficaria verna*
Lesser spearwort = *Ranunculus flammula*
Lesser Twayblade = *Neottia cordata*
Lily of the valley = *Convallaria majalis*
Lizard Orchid = *Himantoglossum hircinum*
Lobelias = *Lobelia spp.*
Loose silky bent = *Apera spica-venti*
Loose-flowered Orchid = *Orchis laxiflora*
Lords-and-ladies = *Arum maculatum*
Love-in-a-mist = *Nigella damascena*
Maiden pink = *Dianthus deltoides*
Male fern = *Dryopteris filix-mas*
Man Orchid = *Aceras anthropophorum*
Marsh bedstraw = *Galium palustre*
Marsh Fragrant Orchid = *Gymnadenia densiflora*
Marsh Helleborine = *Epipactis palustris*
Marsh marigold = *Caltha palustris*
Meadow buttercup = *Ranunculus acris*
Military Orchid = *Orchis militaris*
Monkey Orchid = *Orchis simia*
Moth Orchids = *Phalaenopsis spp.*
Mount Atlas daisy = *Anacyclus pyrethrum*
Mouse-ear hawkweed = *Pilosella officinarum*
Musk Orchid = *Herminium monorchis*
Narrow-leaved Helleborine = *Cephalanthera longifolia*
Narrow-leaved Marsh Orchid = *Dactylorhiza traunsteineri (syn. D. traunsteinerioides)*
Narrow-lipped Helleborine = *Epipactis leptochila*
Nigella = *Nigella damascena*
Northern Marsh Orchid = *Dactylorhiza purpurella*
Ox-eye daisy = *Leucanthemum vulgare*
Pear = *Pyrus communis*
Perennial flax = *Linum perenne*
Pincushion lucida = *Scabiosa lucida*
Pine-pink Orchid = *Bletia purpurea (syn. B. verecunda)*
Pitcher plant = *Sarracenia purpurea*
Plantain lilies = *Hosta spp.*
Pleione Orchids = *Pleione spp.*
Ploughman's spikenard = *Inula conyzae*
Plum = *Prunus domestica*
Primrose = *Primula vulgaris*
Privet = *Ligustrum ovalifolium*
Pyramidal Orchid = *Anacamptis pyramidalis*
Quaking grass = *Briza media*

Ragged robin = *Lychnis flos-cuculi*
Ragwort = *Senecio jacobaea*
Ramsons = *Allium ursinum*
Red clover = *Trifolium pratense*
Red Helleborine = *Cephalanthera rubra*
Rhododendrons = *Rhododendron spp.*
Rhubarbs = *Rheum spp.*
Ribwort plantain = *Plantago lanceolata*
Sassafras = *Sassafras spp.*
Saxifrages = *Saxifraga spp.*
Slipper Orchids = *Paphiopedilum spp.*
Small scabious = *Scabiosa columbaria*
Small White Orchid = *Pseudorchis albida*
Small-flowered Tongue Orchid = *Serapias parviflora*
Snow-in-summer = *Cerastium tomentosum*
Snowdrop = *Galanthus nivalis*
Southern Marsh Orchid = *Dactylorhiza praetermissa*
Spanish bluebell = *Hyacinthoides hispanica*
Spearworts = *Ranunculus spp.*
Squirrel corn = *Dicentra canadensis*
Stiff-flower Star Orchid = *Epidendrum rigidum*
Stinging nettle = *Urtica dioica*
Stokes' aster = *Stokesia laevis*
Stonecrops = *Sedum spp.*
Stream Orchid = *Epipactis gigantea*
Summer Lady's Tresses = *Spiranthes aestivalis*
Sun Orchids = *Thelymitra spp.*
Sundews = *Drosera spp.*
Sweet basil = *Ocimum basilicum*
Sword-leaved Helleborine = *Cephalanthera longifolia*
Sycamore = *Acer pseudoplatanus*
Thistles = *Carduus and Cirsium spp.*
Tormentil = *Potentilla erecta*
Trefoils = *Trifolium spp.*
Tufted vetch = *Vicia cracca*
Tulips = *Tulipa spp.*
Venus Slippers = *Paphiopedilum spp.*
Vetches = *Vicia spp.*
Violet Helleborine = *Epipactis purpurata*
Water buttercups = *Ranunculus spp.*
Water mint = *Mentha aquatica*
White campion = *Silene latifolia*
White Helleborine = *Cephalanthera damasonium*
Wild Garlic = *Allium ursinum*
Wild oat = *Avena fatua*
Wild plum = *Prunus domestica*
Wild thyme = *Thymus polytrichus*
Windowsill Orchid = *Pleione formosana*
Wood anemone = *Anemone nemorosa*
Wood sorrel = *Oxalis acetosella*
Yellow rattle = *Rhinanthus minor*
Young's Helleborine = *Epipactis youngiana*

PLANT LIST 2: LATIN TO COMMON NAMES

Acer palmatum = Japanese maple
Acer pseudoplatanus = Sycamore
Aceras anthropophorum = Man Orchid
Achillea tomentosa = Alpine yarrow
Adiantum venustum = Evergreen maidenhair
Adiantum venustum = Himalayan maidenhair
Aesculus hippocastanum = Horse chestnut
Ajuga reptans = Bugle
Allium ursinum = Ramsons
Allium ursinum = Wild garlic
Anacamptis morio = Green-veined Orchid
Anacamptis morio = Green-winged Orchid
Anacamptis pyramidalis = Pyramidal Orchid
Anacyclus pyrethrum = Mount Atlas daisy
Anemone nemorosa = Wood anemone
Anthyllis vulneraria = Kidney vetch
Apera spica-venti = Loose silky-bent
Artocarpus altilis = Breadfruit
Arum italicum = Italian lords-and-ladies
Arum maculatum = Cuckoo pint
Arum maculatum = Lords-and-ladies
Aubrieta species = Aubretia
Avena fatua = Wild-oat
Bletia purpurea = Pine-pink Orchid
Bletia verecunda = Pine-pink Orchid
Briza media = Quaking grass
Campanula species = Bellflower
Cardamine pratensis = Cuckooflower
Cardamine pratensis = Lady's smock
Carduus species = Thistle
Carex flacca = Glaucous sedge
Catanache caerulea = Blue cupidone
Catanache caerulea = Blue daisy
Cattleya labiate = Cattleya
Centaurea cyanus = Annual cornflower
Centaurea cyanus = Cornflower
Centaurea nigra = Common knapweed
Centaurea scabiosa = Greater knapweed
Cephalanthera damasonium = White Helleborine
Cephalanthera longifolia = Narrow-leaved Helleborine
Cephalanthera longifolia = Sword-leaved Helleborine
Cephalanthera rubra = Red Helleborine
Cerastium tomentosum = Snow-in-summer
Cirsium species = Thistle
Coeloglossum viride = Frog Orchid
Convallaria majalis = Lily-of-the-valley
Corallorhiza trifida = Coralroot Orchid
Coriandrum sativum = Coriander
Corylus avellana = Hazel
Crataegus monogyna = Hawthorn
Cynosurus cristatus = Crested dog's-tail
Cypripedium calceolus = Lady's Slipper Orchid

Dactylorhiza ebudensis = Hebridean Marsh Orchid
Dactylorhiza fuchsii = Common Spotted Orchid
Dactylorhiza incarnata = Early Marsh Orchid
Dactylorhiza maculata = Heath Spotted Orchid
Dactylorhiza praetermissa = Southern Marsh Orchid
Dactylorhiza purpurella = Dwarf Purple Orchid
Dactylorhiza purpurella = Northern Marsh Orchid
Dactylorhiza species = Marsh Orchid
Dactylorhiza species = Spotted Orchid
Dactylorhiza traunsteineri = Narrow-leaved Marsh Orchid
Dactylorhiza traunsteinerioides = Narrow-leaved Marsh Orchid
Dactylorhiza traunsteinerioides subsp. Lapponica = Lapland Marsh Orchid
Dactylorhiza viridis = Frog Orchid
Dianthus armeria = Deptford pink
Dianthus deltoides = Maiden pink
Dianthus species = Carnation
Dianthus species = Pink
Dicentra canadensis = Squirrel corn
Dicentra cucullaria = Dutchman's breeches
Digitalis purpurea = Foxglove
Drosera species = Sundew
Dryopteris filix-mas = Male-fern
Epidendrum rigidum = Stiff-flower Star Orchid
Epipactis atrorubens = Dark-red Helleborine
Epipactis dunensis = Dune Helleborine
Epipactis gigantea = Stream Orchid
Epipactis helleborine = Broad-leaved Helleborine
Epipactis leptochila = Narrow-lipped Helleborine
Epipactis palustris = Marsh Helleborine
Epipactis phyllanthes = Green-flowered Helleborine
Epipactis purpurata = Violet Helleborine
Epipactis species = Helleborine
Epipactis youngiana = Young's Helleborine
Epipogium aphyllum = Ghost Orchid
Eriophorum angustifolium = Common cottongrass
Euphrasia officinalis agg. = Eyebright
Ficaria verna = Lesser celandine
Galanthus nivalis = Snowdrop
Galium palustre = Marsh bedstraw
Galium uliginosum = Fen bedstraw
Geranium robertianum = Herb-Robert
Goodyera repens = Creeping lady's-tresses
Gunnera species = Giant rhubarb
Gymnadenia borealis = Heath Fragrant Orchid
Gymnadenia conopsea = Chalk Fragrant Orchid
Gymnadenia conopsea = Common Fragrant Orchid
Gymnadenia densiflora = Marsh Fragrant Orchid
Gymnadenia species = Fragrant Orchid
Hammarbya paludosa = Bog Orchid
Helianthemum nummularium = Common rock-rose

Herminium monorchis = Musk Orchid
Himantoglossum hircinum = Lizard Orchid
Hosta crispula = Curled plantain lily
Hosta species = Hosta
Hosta species = Plantain lily
Hyacinthoides hispanica = Spanish bluebell
Hyacinthoides non-scripta = Bluebell
Inula conyzae = Ploughman's-spikenard
Knautia arvensis = Field scabious
Leontodon species = Hawkbit
Leucanthemum vulgare = Oxeye daisy
Ligustrum ovalifolium = Garden privet
Ligustrum ovalifolium = Privet
Linum perenne = Blue flax
Linum perenne = Perennial flax
Liparis loeselii = Fen Orchid
Lobelia cardinalis = Cardinal flower
Lobelia species = Lobelia
Lychnis flos-cuculi = Ragged robin
Lysimachia nummularia = Creeping Jenny
Malus pumila = Apple
Malus pumila 'Egremont Russet' = 'Egremont Russet' Apple
Medicago lupulina = Black medick
Miltonia vexillaria = [No common name]
Neotinea maculata = Dense-flowered Orchid
Neottia cordata = Lesser Twayblade
Neottia nidus-avis = Bird's-nest Orchid
Neottia ovata = Common Twayblade
Nigella damascena = Love-in-a-mist
Ocimum basilicum = Basil
Ocimum basilicum = Sweet Basil
Odontoglossum crispum = Curled Odontoglossum
Ononis repens = Common restharrow
Ophrys apifera = Bee Orchid
Ophrys fuciflora = Late Spider Orchid
Ophrys insectifera = Fly Orchid
Ophrys sphegodes = Early Spider Orchid
Orchis laxiflora = Loose-flowered Orchid
Orchis mascula = Early Purple Orchid
Orchis militaris = Military Orchid
Orchis simia = Monkey Orchid
Orchis ustulata = Burnt Orchid
Oxalis acetosella = Wood-sorrel
Papaver rhoeas = Common poppy
Paphiopedilum = Slipper Orchid
Paphiopedilum = Venus Slipper
Phalaenopsis species = Moth Orchid
Pilosella = Hawkweed
Pilosella officinarum = Mouse-ear hawkweed
Pinguicula species = Butterwort
Plantago lanceolata = Ribwort plantain
Plantago major = Greater plantain
Platanthera bifolia = Lesser Butterfly Orchid
Platanthera chlorantha = Greater Butterfly Orchid

Platanthera species = Butterfly Orchid
Pleione = Pleione
Pleione formosana = Windowsill Orchid
Poa annua = Annual meadow-grass
Polypogon monspeliensis = Annual beard-grass
Potentilla erecta = Tormentil
Primula veris = Cowslip
Primula vulgaris = Primrose
Prunus domestica = Plum
Prunus domestica = Wild plum
Pseudorchis albida = Small White Orchid
Pteridium aquilinum = Bracken
Pyrus communis = European pear
Pyrus communis = Pear
Ranunculus acris = Meadow buttercup
Ranunculus flammula = Lesser spearwort
Ranunculus species = Spearwort
Ranunculus species = Water buttercup
Rheum species = Rhubarb
Rhinanthus minor = Yellow rattle
Rhododendron species = Rhododendron
Rubus caesius = Dewberry
Rubus fruticosus agg. = Bramble
Rumex obtusifolius = Broad-leaved dock
Salix repens = Creeping willow
Sarracenia purpurea = Pitcherplant
Sarracenia species = Pitcher plant
Sassafras species = Sassafras
Saxifraga species = Saxifrage
Scabiosa lucida = Pincushion lucida
Sedum species = Stonecrop
Sempervivum species = Houseleek
Senecio jacobaea = Common ragwort
Senecio jacobaea = Ragwort
Serapias lingua = Greater Tongue Orchid
Serapias parviflora = Small-flowered Tongue Orchid
Silene latifolia = White campion
Sisyrinchium bellum = Blue-eyed grass
Spiranthes aestivalis = Summer lady's-tresses
Spiranthes romanzoffiana = Irish lady's-tresses
Spiranthes spiralis = Autumn lady's-tresses
Stellaria holostea = Greater stitchwort
Stokesia laevis = Stokes' aster
Succisa pratensis = Devil's-bit scabious
Taraxacum officinale agg. = Dandelion
Thelymitra species = Sun Orchid
Thymus polytrichus = Wild thyme
Trifolium pratense = Red clover
Trifolium species = Trefoil
Tulipa species = Tulip
Ulex europaeus = Gorse
Urtica dioica = Common nettle
Urtica dioica = Nettle
Vicia cracca = Tufted vetch
Vicia species = Vetch

Resources

Suppliers

Orchid Plants

Bewdley Orchid supplies ready-to-plant British orchids grown from ethically sourced seed. www.bewdleyorchids.com

Laneside Hardy Orchids sells plants for garden or meadow. **www.lanesidehardyorchids.com**

Orchid Meadow supplies orchid plant for the garden on a seasonal basis. **www.orchidmeadow.co.uk**

Crocus sells a few hardy *Bletia* species. **www.crocus.co.uk**

Heritage Orchids sells some hardy *Pleiones* suitable for the garden. **www.heritageorchids.co.uk**

Wildflowers can be bought in plugs from British Wild Flower Plants at **www.wildflowers.co.uk**

Spicesotic Plants have hardy plants for sale on a seasonal basis. **www.spicesotic.co.uk**

Phytesia, based in Belgium, sells hardy orchids to commercial outlets. **www.phytesia.com**

Orchid Seeds

If you buy seeds they need to be started off in culture.

Manomano sell Common Spotted Orchid seed at **www.manomano.co.uk**

Wild flower Lawns and Meadows have orchid seed for sale **www.wildflowerlawnsandmeadows.com**

Growth Media for Seeds

Sigma-Aldrich supply Phytamax & Knudson C **www.sigmaaldrich.com**

Himedia sell Knudson C, Malmgren's, Murashige and Skoog, and Mitra. **www.himedialabs.com**

A range of media solutions are available from **www.kay-orchid-flask-factory.com**

General Equipment

Ashwood Nurseries have a wide selection of containers of all sorts and an area which they are developing as a meadow. **www.ashwoodnurseries.com**

Vertical laminar flow cabinets are available from Monmouth Scientific (**www.monmouthscientific.co.uk**), or Camlab (**www.camlab.co.uk**).

Used and refurbished equipment can be purchased from Akribis Scientific Ltd (**www.akribis.co.uk**)

For autoclaves and cabinets Wolflabs have a considerable range at **www.wolflabs.co.uk**

For autoclaves you can use a domestic pressure cooker, these tend to have a smaller capacity than laboratory autoclaves, but are just as good for small volumes.

Scythes

Power scythes are ideal for annual meadow cuts and control of invasive species such as brambles. Hire locally or buy from **www.lawnflite.co.uk** or **www.tracmaster.co.uk**

The Scythe Shop supplies hand scythes along with advice. **www.thescytheshop.co.uk**

Wildflower seed and plants

Although the dates can vary year to year, specialist plant fairs provide well grown specimens of plants suitable for introduction into meadows or woods. Plant fairs can be found at **www.rareplantfair.co.uk** and **www.planthuntersfairs.co.uk**

Boston Seeds provide a wide range of both perennials and annuals, which are sold by weight. They also sell plug plants for ground cover, like wood anemones, **www.bostonseeds.com**

Meadow Mania sells seeds by weight as mixtures categorized by soil type. **www.meadowmania.co.uk**

Meadow Mat can provide seeds for smaller areas. **www.meadowmat.com**

Annuals and perennials are available from the social enterprise **www.wildflower.org.uk**

Really Wild Flowers sell wild flower seed in small quantities at **www.reallywildflowers.co.uk**

Wild Flower Lawns and Meadows sell wild flower seed and supply Yellow Rattle seed in large quantities. **www.wildflowerlawnsandmeadows.com**

Wildflower Shop sells plug plants which are suitable both for woodlands and meadows. **www.wildflowershop.co.uk**

Naturescape can provide a range of plants for ground cover, like violets. **www.naturescape.co.uk**

A wide range of plants for growing under trees, many of them not native, are available from **www.plantsforshade.co.uk**

Plants for all sites can be provided by Plant Wild at **www.plantwild.co.uk**

Specialist Plant Nurseries

Native and non-native carnivorous plants are available from P and J Plants **www.pj.plants.co.uk**, also Hewitt-Cooper Carnivorous Plants at **www.hccarnivorousplants.co.uk** and Little Shop of Horrors, **www.littleshopofhorrors.co.uk**

Hostas are available from Bowden Hostas, **www.bowdenhostas.com** and Mickfield Hostas **www.mickfieldhostas.co.uk**

Ferns can be purchased from The Fern Nursery, **www.fernnursery.co.uk** and Plants For Shade at **www.plantsforshade.co.uk**

Societies

Hardy Orchid Society. **www.hardyorchidsociety.org.uk**

Hardy Plant Society. A more general society for hardy plant enthusiasts. **www.hardy-plant.org.uk**

Orchid Society of Great Britain. A Society for orchid enthusiasts of all sorts, but mainly of tropical and sub-tropical species. **www.osbg.org.uk**

Plantlife International. **www.plantlife.org.uk**

Flora Locale promotes the restoration of wild plants for biodiversity **www.floralocale.org**

Botanical Society of the British Isles (BSBI). **www.bsbi.org.uk.** For details of distribution of species, on the Home page click on Resources and then maps.

Campaign to Protect Rural England (CPRE). **www.cpre.org.uk**

The Cottage Garden Society, helping traditional methods of cottage gardening. **www.thecgs.org.uk** Natural England **www.natural-england.org.uk**

The Alpine Garden Society for growers of alpine plants. **www.alpinegardensociety.net.**

The Woodland Trust. **www.woodland-trust.org.uk**

A list of UK smallholder groups can be found at **www.smallplotbigideas.co.uk**

If you have a piece of old garden or farm machinery you may find help in finding spare parts and maintenance at the Farm Machinery Preservation Society, **www.fmps.org.uk** or at the Vintage Garden Machinery Club, **www.vhgmc.co.uk**

Help with woodland care is contained in Living Woods Magazine, **www.livingwoodsmagazine.co.uk**

A very interesting place to learn about scythes is the Scythe Association, **www.scytheassociation.org**

Books of interest and further reading

Amherst, Alicia *A History of Gardening in England* (1895)

Bates, H.E *Through The Woods* (2011) reprint Little Toller Books, Dorset

Dickinson, Tracy *Wild Flowers* (2003) Green Books

Edwards, M. and Jenner, M. *Field Guide to the Bumble-bees of Britain and Ireland* (2005) Ocelli Publishing

Goulson, D. *A Buzz in the Meadow* (2014) Jonathan Cape, London

Hickin, Norman *The Natural History of an English Forest: The wild life of Wyre*

Higgins, L.G. and Riley, N.D. *A field Guide to the Butterflies of Britain and Europe* (1980) Collins, London

Jefferies, Richard *The Life of the Fields* (1884)

Kodicek & Young Captain Cook and Scurvy (1969): **https://www.jstor.org/stable/530740?seq=1#page_scan_tab_contents**

Lang, D. Britain's *Orchids* (2004) Wild Guides Ltd, Hampshire

Mabey, Richard *Flora Britannica* (1996)

Millican, Albert *Travels and Adventures of an Orchid Hunter* (1891)

Report on the Orchid Conference 1885. Journal of the Royal Horticultural Society. VII (1) 1886

Sterry, P. *Collins Complete Guide to British Wild Flowers* (2006) HarperCollins, London

Summerhayes, V.S. *Wild Orchids of Britain* (2009) (reprint) Harper Collins, London

Verner, Yvette *The English Meadow* (2008) Green Books

Verner, Yvette *Creating a Wildflower Meadow* (new edition due 2019) Green Books

Webster, A.D. *British Orchids* (1898) J.S Virtue &Co, London

2016 British Wildlife report on the fields of County Mayo: **https://media.nhbs.com/bw/British-wildlife-Feb2016-vol27-no3-digital.pdf**

Index

ALSO BY GREEN BOOKS

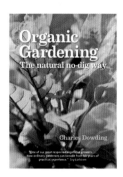

Organic Gardening
CHARLES DOWDING
The guru of no-dig gardening shows how to grow a delicious variety of fruit and vegetables organically: what to choose; when to sow, plant and harvest; and how to avoid pests and disease.

The Garden Awakening
MARY REYNOLDS
Create beautiful, vibrant and magical spaces with growing food and living sustainably at its heart. View the land with the eyes of a parent: nurture it, love it, help it fulfil its own truth and restore its harmony and energy.

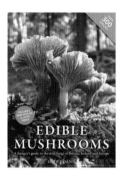

Edible Mushrooms
GEOFF DANN
Featuring over 300 edible species, describing the best tasting ones, where to find them and when they are at their best, this is a book for both beginners and experienced foragers.

Creating a Forest Garden
MARTIN CRAWFORD
Grow edible crops using permaculture principles and letting nature do most of the work. This is the definitive book on Forest Gardening.

The Fruit Tree Handbook
BEN PIKE
A clear, practical guide for both amateur and expert that explains all you need to know to grow delicious fruit, from designing your orchard and planting your trees to harvesting your produce.

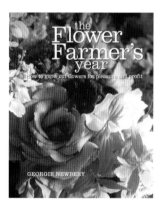

The Flower Farmer's Year
GEORGIE NEWBURY
Grow your own scented flowers that will feed the bees and grow in a vase. Make a haven for hedgehogs, toads, and birds that feed on the slugs, snails and other plant predators in your organic cut-flower garden.

About Green Books

green books

Environmental publishers for 25 years.

For our full range of titles and to order direct from our website, see **www.greenbooks.co.uk**

Join our mailing list for new titles, special offers, reviews, author appearances and events: **www.greenbooks.co.uk/subscribe**

For bulk orders (50+ copies) we offer discount terms. Contact **sales@greenbooks.co.uk** for details.

Send us a book proposal on eco-building, science, gardening, etc.: see **www.greenbooks.co.uk/for-authors**

 @ Green_Books   /GreenBooks